D1186780

TAMARA DREWE

SWINDON COLLEGE

LEARNING RESOURCE CENTRE

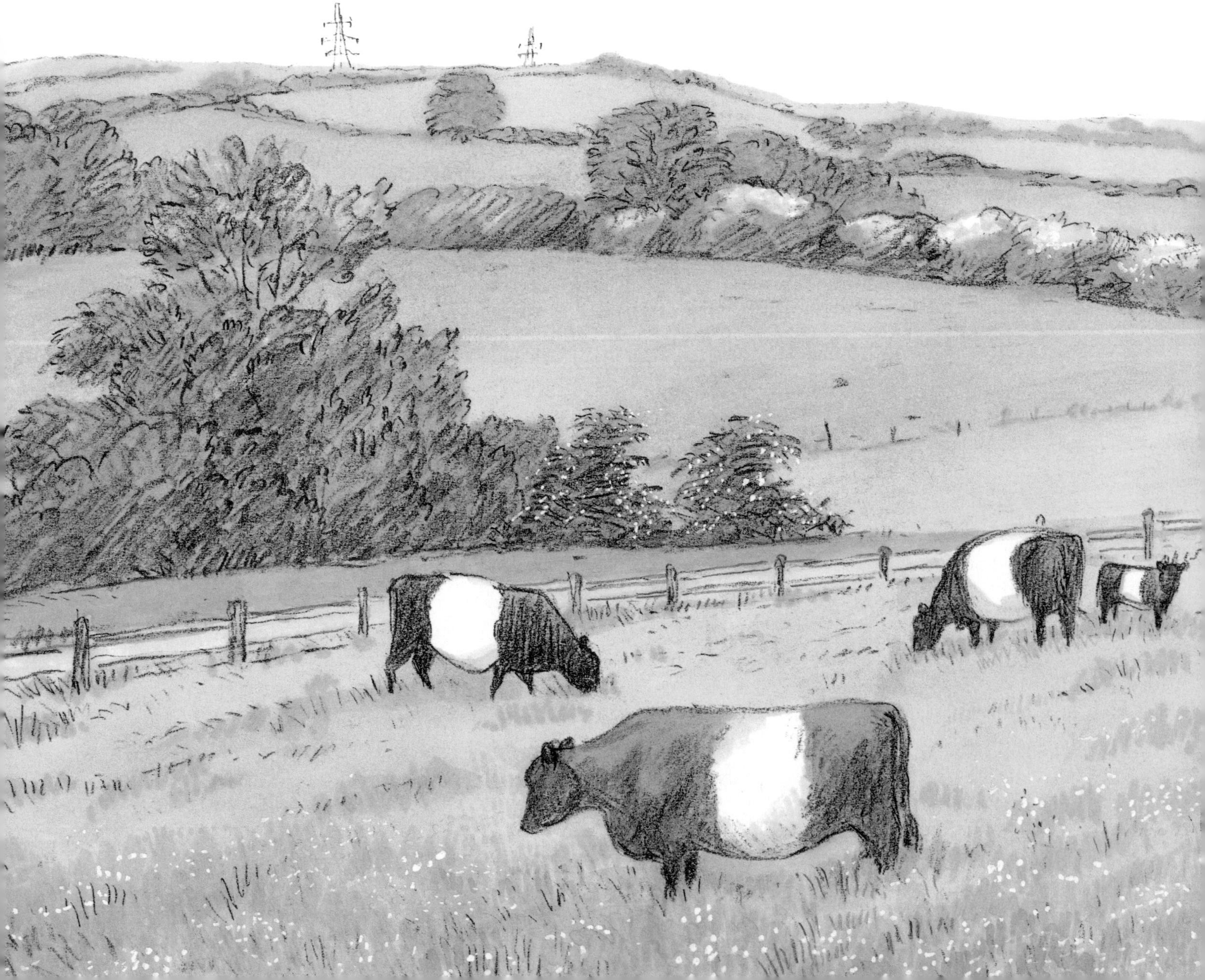

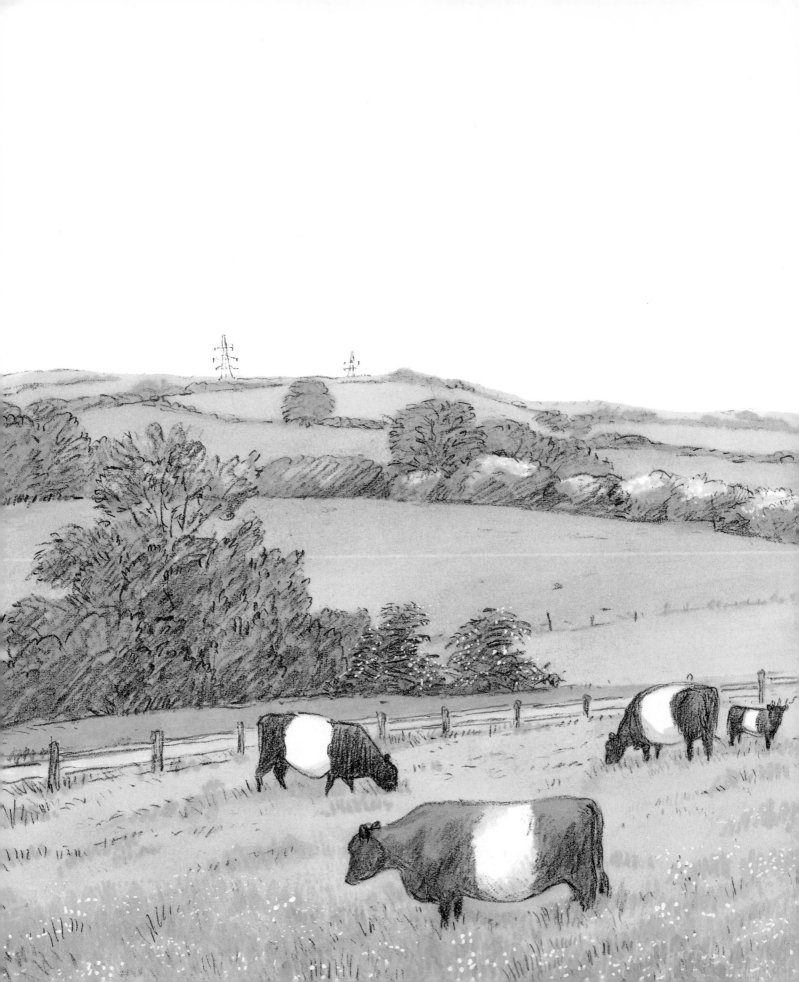

TAMARA DREWE

Posy Simmonds

SWINDON COLLEGE

LEARNING RESOURCE CENTRE

JONATHAN CAPE
LONDON

5405000379362

2nd FEBRUARY 2012

First published by Jonathan Cape in 2007
This trade paperback edition published by Jonathan Cape in 2009

4 6 8 10 9 7 5 3

Copyright © Posy Simmonds 2007

Posy Simmonds has asserted her right under the Copyright, Designs
and Patents Act 1988 to be identified as the author of this work

This book is sold subject to the condition that it shall not,
by way of trade or otherwise, be lent, resold, hired out,or otherwise circulated
without the publisher's prior consent in any form of binding or cover other than that
in which it is published and without a similar condition including this condition
being imposed on the subsequent purchaser

First published in cartoon strip form in the *Guardian*

First published in book form in Great Britain in 2007 by
Jonathan Cape
Random House, 20 Vauxhall Bridge Road,
London SW1V 2SA

The Random House Group Limited Reg. No. 954009

A CIP catalogue record for this book is available from the British Library

ISBN 9780224078177

The Random House Group Limited makes every effort to ensure that the papers used in its books
are made from trees that have been legally sourced from well-managed and credibly certified forests.
Our paper procurement policy can be found at: www.randomhouse.co.uk/paper.htm

Printed and bound in Italy by Conti Tipocolor S.p.A., Florence

SWINDON COLLEGE

LEARNING RESOURCE CENTRE

To Richard

TAMARA DREWE

AUGUST

Fairy-tale Cottage. Writer's retreat. Secluded furnished cottage. Oak beams. Open fire. Sleeps 1. Ideal for complete solitude. "A place for writing at every window". £300 p.w. available monthly basis. No pets. Tel/fax 010935 709 4210.

Far from the Madding Crowd. Working retreat for writers. Easy access M96. Great scenery, good walking. Eight quiet, comfortable studios in converted farm buildings. Long or short lets. Communal evening meal provided in main house. No obligation to socialise. Laundry service. Typing/word processing service available, from m/s to hard copy or disk by confidential, qualified secretary. e-mail stonefield@easymail.com

Rural Gite. Tranquil location near Albi. 15 minutes walk from pretty village. Available for short term rental. Terrace and large garden. Images on http//www. AlicaciaPralley.net

American
Portreath
QT. Email:

author / ex-
ft ready for
available for
subject too
4210 or write
31 5SL.

one bderoom
Translation/
able. Email
oorman.com

Welsh) young
or

Writing / Resea
editor will revi
for synopsis ar

Book Find Se
Send list of w
to 8935 Pont
Email: orders

Writing / Res
editor will re
publication. l
research, gh
recondite. T
write 23 Bul

Pisa, Histc
apartment a
rental. Suit
Images on
forestino.ne

rth Cornwall. Charmi

COK COK...

COK-KARK!

EWEDOWN

!?!*

Assholes!

O come on, Glen...they're just bored...holidays've gone on too long...just mindless...

But that's what I object to! I mean if they threw stuff with a *purpose*...like they see us and think: **hey**, writers! let's egg the self-regarding sacks of shit...

Maybe they did...

Sure, Beth, don't bother... I know my way around.

OK...well the key's in the door.

Thanks for picking me up

My pleasure.... Now, drinks at half six...see you later

Stonefield Retreat

Dr Glen Larson, translator (MFA, University of Arkansas, PhD, Columbia, currently Visiting Professor at London Medial University).

Glen Larson: **M**y second time at Stonefield. I tried a week here at Easter and decided it might do for a month or two of the sabbatical I'd wangled. (My "bloody skive" as colleagues call it.)

Last time I was in a different barn, in a room called Garsington. Now I'm in Bateman's, near the main house. It's a hot afternoon. I switch on the fan, help myself from the little icebox, put my feet up, and sigh in disgust.

Disgust at Stonefield? This might seem perverse, especially if you compare it with my toxic London neighborhood or with the other retreats I've tried: in Andalucia (power blackouts, mosquitoes); in Yorkshire (screeching firedoors, curried lasagne, rooms that froze your balls off).

I guess my problem with Stonefield is the luxury, the brazen comfort. There's something absolutely corrupting about the goosedown pillows, fine percale bedsheets, the cozy armchairs, log fires, the voluptuous loungers in shady spots, the really great food and wine. All this makes me uneasy. I mean, should a writer live like a pig in shit and expect the Muse to call?

Beth Hardiman runs the place so discreetly and efficiently, everything laid on. It's like having servants, and that's kind of noxious too. I feel she should ask us writers at least to pick up a dishcloth, but she never does. "You've got better things to do," she'll say. Beth of course is a rare woman, one who understands the creative process – the preoccupation, the long hours of brooding.

So OK, Stonefield has its positive aspects: obviously the seclusion, the deep, deep hush and, going by my last visit, no one here I couldn't happily ignore. My fellow scribes will be pretty much the same, quiet and tippy-toed, middle class, over thirty-five, no one needy or deprived, like in London. In other words, absolutely no one to feel bad about.

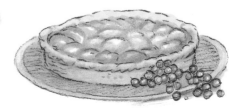

Beth Hardiman:

The egg, very likely from one of our hens, has baked dry on the car. Some of it just flakes off, the rest I take a wet sponge to.
God, the sun's hot, hotter than ever. Inside, the house is cool enough, but I begin to worry about everyone in the barns. We have six writers in residence . . .

D'you think they're roasting, Mary?

Think I should be reminding them to drink enough?

Noo! Beth, *really!* They're not invalids!

You worry too much

Well, someone has to worry, running a place like Stonefield. You have constantly to think of the hazards: fire, salmonella, writers tripping, scalding, electrocuting themselves. Anyway, at least we can't be blamed for the heatwave.

I think of my husband Nicholas in the Shed. He can write eight pages a day whatever the weather. Strangely, in the past few weeks he hasn't. When I've gone as usual to collect the day's work, there's been nothing to take for typing. Just Nicholas, looking all stuck and broody. I suggested it must be the hot weather. He agreed, probably it was, but I don't believe that's the reason. I know about writer's block but I also know not to call it by name. Oh, I feel for Nicholas. This book should have been ready for the Christmas market, but for the first time ever he's missed all the deadlines. I imagine him cooped up in the Shed, agonising over a phrase or, more likely, staring out at the view.

Nadia! Why you doing this!?

You're putting me off!...You **are**! Darling, I *must* see you! We **have** to talk.....yes...yes, I *mean* it!

No, tomorrow's no good! I *told* you, it's difficult...

OK! OK! Tomorrow then...I'll just have to think of something....

The next day is cooler, which is just as well. We're going to a party in London and staying overnight in the flat. Our daughter has moved in there and seeing her will be the one positive aspect of the trip. Otherwise a big pain. Not just the drive, but all the bother beforehand: getting Andy to do the poultry, asking Mary to stay here and take charge. (She never minds, but her husband does. He told her I exploit her.)

I don't have anything towny to wear and don't much care. All the same, I've nothing that fits or that disguises the flab I've put on. Only a linen suit. In the mirror I loom large, black and white like a killer whale.

Nicholas has been ready for over an hour. Three or four times he comes in the bedroom, bristling with tension. But we aren't late. There's ample time for the journey; the party is for a modest-selling author, so little risk of Nick feeling outshone. On the contrary, he'll be lionised, be able to flirt and charm. He'll hear the gossip. I'll drive, so he can drink . . . What's eating him?

Is that what you're wearing?

Yes...why? What's wrong with it?

Nothing...it's just not very summery... Won't you be hot in that jacket?

I've got to wear it. What's the matter? You've seen it loads of times...Suddenly you hate it!

I don't hate it...I didn't say that...it's just a bit hot-looking...

All right! All right! I'll take it OFF!!

No, don't Beth! It's fine! I shouldn't have said anything!

Ignore me!

If you didn't say anything you'd still *think* it...

Not wearing it!...Throw the bloody thing in the bin!

But you looked *fine*!

Actually, Nicholas... I can't do this...I'm fed up...I'm not going.... You go on your own...

Do! Go on, I don't want to go...

I mean it, Nick... You go...you'll enjoy it...I won't .

OK

If that's what you really want

It's the way he says the last thing rather too quickly, the way he scoops up and catches the car keys. I suddenly twig. He's engineered this. He's never wanted me to go and leaving me behind has been a piece of cake. If I don't feel I look right I tend to back out of things. As well he knows.

Why doesn't Nicholas want me to be with him in London? Am I too fat and dowdy to be seen with? Or is he ill? Has he gone to learn he has terminal cancer? Is he buying my birthday present? Or is he seeing someone? *Yes.* He's seeing a woman, and that explains everything, why he can't work. He's having an affair! Which wouldn't be the first time. But in the past I've always known about his bits on the side, because he's more or less told me. That's our understanding: a blind eye in return for being honest. *He always tells me that I'm the centre of his life. That he can't do without me.* Why is he being so bloody devious?

I shut myself in the bedroom and stayed there. (Thank God, Mary was on hand for the writers.) After a terrible night I'm up at 5, cooking. No word from Nicholas. At first I'd expected him to turn back or to ring from the end of the drive, or at least from London. Usually after one of our rare spats he would clear the air immediately; sulking uses up too much of his creative energy.

This time it's serious. I know our marriage is as good as over, that I've been a bloody fool, that never in 25 years have I handled things so badly. Screaming at him, forcing him to choose between me and ... *Who the hell is she?* Will Nicholas already have told our daughter? Should I e-mail our son Fred, backpacking in Queensland. What would I say? "Dad and I are splitting up. He's left me for another ... "

And then the embarrassment here at Stonefield. Unforgiveably, yesterday we disturbed the writers' peace. Everyone must have overheard. Andy Cobb certainly had. When he comes in with the veg this morning he launches straight into it. I'm sure he means to be kind and supportive. Fond as I am of him, I can't stand it.

...he doesn't know he's lucky...things you do for him, Beth...

He won't last five minutes without you... you'll see...

I'll be getting along, then...

You be all right, Beth?

Yes

Thanks, Andy

But Andy is right. When I thought of all I do for Nick (voluntarily, it has to be said): *I* run the household, manage the writers, and our 16 acres. *I* deal with the children and our employees, Andy and Mary. *I* look after the bills, the accounts, the VAT, the leasing of the fields and the piles of government bumf. Does Nick *ever* have to worry about the hedges or the new subsidy system?

I give Nick peace and freedom to write. And that's not all. *I* transform his grubby longhand into double-spaced typescripts. *I* edit, research, contribute to plots, make his female characters convincing, suggest names and titles ('Doctor Inchcombe' was *my* invention). Above all, I act as his gatekeeper. It's me who keeps his public sweet, who replies to fans, charities, students, tyro authors and time wasters. I even forge his signature.

If Nicholas Hardiman's public thinks him decent, charming and generous, then it's my doing. He couldn't do without me, could he?

Beth screaming at her husband, that was a shock, also a pain in the ass. She totally screwed my concentration.

Up to that moment I'd been doing great: the morning working on a translation, and the afternoon on my biographical novel about Verlaine (fourth draft). Then the Hardimans' row, which immediately reminded me of another, a scene I'd been trying to forget. Well, it wasn't much of a row, just Maggie's quiet Scotch voice, more sorrow than anger. Only ten days before. . .

NO! It's no good, Glen!

I've wasted 2 years of my life waiting for you to stop avoiding the issue...

I'm 36...I'm not waiting anymore

When I come back from my trip, I don't expect to find you here...

uh...so soon?.. uh.. Finding somewhere will...uh...maybe I could stay just...?

No, I want you gone! Before I get back...I want you to go!

Maggie...I never...I...if I'd known you felt that way, I'd.....*God,* I mean you said you never wanted them, remember?...you said your career..... uh, I mean, this is just awful...I...

The next day Maggie went off on her field trip, studying inter-tidal life or whatever, leaving me to move out of her apartment. Well, to move my things a few feet out of the bedroom into the spare room that Maggie was indulgent or dumb or cunning enough to suggest I used as a store, until I found somewhere else. Maybe her intention was to hold my books and winter knits as hostages; maybe she held out the hope of luring me back.

To be honest, the split is a relief. I like Maggie, but don't love her, or not enough to commit long term. Marriage, kids. I mean I already have an ex-wife in the States, thankfully remarried.

Besides, Maggie's and my relationship grew out of mutual convenience: her apartment was handy for the university and my rent eased the pain of her mortgage. We were buddies. OK, we had some polite bedding, but I saw myself as really more lodger than lover.

I was this model guy sharing the chores, respecting her career, encouraging her climb up the academic tree. Then suddenly I'm this pig, this total bastard denying her the right to a baby-buggy in the hall.

I sit there feeling terrible again and get no further with Verlaine, beside whose heroic debauchery I am, I guess, a real pantyhose.

It's 9am the next morning. I'm in the toilet, the one nobody uses much, near the side door of Stonefield House. It has books, framed photos of Nicholas Hardiman's triumphs and, most importantly, a solid, loadbearing toilet. I prefer not to use the nifty cantilevered ones in the writers' bathrooms, for reasons fellow fatsos will understand. Indeed, as Beth Hardiman understood when showing me my room, the first time I stayed here. I only had to eye the toilet for her to pick up immediately.

"Oh, and by the way, Glen," she said, "there are two downstairs loos in the main house. Feel free to use them." And so I do. But as it's kind of gross going into someone's house just to take a dump, I time my visits, to sneak in and out without being seen. I'm pretty sure Beth is upstairs in the tub, and as for Nicholas – well, he's just left her, for God's sake! Or rather, Beth kicked him out, as we couldn't help overhearing. And couldn't help discussing last night. Me, two novelists and the gardener guy, Andy. We walked down the road to the Rick, which, as Andy never tires of telling me, was once a nice old pub, the Stag and Hounds.

Let's eat in the garden!

...but giving him an ultimatum! Making him choose: *her* or the mistress! Bit rash, don't you think?

Nick might not come back...

I'd have him back...

But maybe that's what Beth wants...

I wouldn't! He's much too up himself!

I suppose if they divorce, they'd have to sell Stonefield ...split the difference...

God, Andy! You could be out of a job!

Look, can we sort of shut up about this? ....Beth's a friend...She's been very good to me...

Oh sorry, Andy

So there I am, still in the toilet, realising it's not going to be a great day for translating Benjamin Péret. Thanks to those several bottles of Coonawarra, the duck-fat chunky chips, the rum raisin crème brulée and the gooey chocolate thing I helped Andy finish. When I next raise my head, it's because there are footsteps right outside on the gravel and through the frosted glass I can just make out . . . my God, Nicholas Hardiman!

Very quickly it becomes clear: the scene of the Hardimans' reunion (or, who knows, their final split?) is going to be in the lobby just a few feet away from the toilet where I'm heaving my pants up and thinking wildly of escape. The sensible thing would be to warn them I'm here. Luckily it's a violent, old-fangled toilet with a flush like Niagara Falls and a great gargling suck-away: ERRRRHRRKK. Plenty loud enough. Then, unbolt the door, excuse myself, cut and run. That's my plan. But I'm too slow. I'm still fumbling with my zipper when outside the door Beth's voice stops me dead.

"So?" she says sternly. "No, don't touch me, don't you dare." And Nicholas says, not in his usual, measured (and I have to say, condescending) tone, but in a hoarse, ragged voice (and it's horrible to overhear):

"Oh Beth, I'm sorry, really sorry. I don't know how you'll ever forgive me."

"Nicholas, who is she?"

"You mean? Ah. Nadia Patel. We met at Bentons. She does foreign rights. She was important to me. I won't lie."

"She was important and now she's not. So that's all right then, Nick, is it?"

"Beth, don't make it so difficult!"

"ME?! You, Nicholas, you bloody make things difficult! Yesterday you as good as told me you wanted to live with her."

"I didn't know what I was saying . . . all the way to London I thought and thought. By the time I saw . . . "

"You saw her at the party?"

"No. At her place. I said . . I told her, that was it. I wanted things to end."

"So what did she have to say?"

"Erm. She was upset. She thought it was for the best."

"How touching," Beth says.

Now there's the sound of her sobbing. It's just awful. And Nick's voice, barely audible, coaxing and comforting. And then silences, during which I ease the bolt free and take a peek or two. After what seems like a month, Beth says, not in an unfriendly way, "Look, I must take the empties to the Bottle Bank," and Nick says, quite urgently. "And we'll talk later, won't we? I love you."

I wait. I hear a car leaving, someone sighing, feet scuffing on the gravel. A mobile rings. There are hurried footsteps towards the house. The back door shuts. Nicholas's voice outside the goddam toilet again.

 Now it's safe to come out. I'm thinking, "Ho, ho. Macho pride. What a liar, telling Beth he's given his girlfriend the push when *she'd* kicked *him* out. That's why he's back with his tail between his legs. My my, naughty Nicholas!"

Even before these events, I thought of Nicholas, if I'd thought about him at all, as an asshole. "Arsehole", as he would say. A snitty British arsehole. It's the way at dinner he always defers to me as an academic, as a writer of Literature, i.e., a salaried idler and writer of stuff no one reads – don't think I haven't picked that up.

Nicholas never, ever mentions his own success, his sales, advances, and myriad TV adaptions. He doesn't have to; it is understood. If I ask him about his work he invites me to despise it, "Just a way of earning a crust", he'll say. "Of no account, of no lasting value. Not like your work, Glen". Meaning my pathetic output. Nicholas maintains that writing his sort of book is a breeze, whereas mine demands years of effort. (I have actually read one of his books and surprisingly agree with the garbage on the back cover. It was "intelligently written", I'll give him that.)

But Nicholas likes to show off to women, especially the tyro writers (and Stonefield attracts a lot of those). Several times I've overheard him spouting on the hard graft, discipline and loneliness of writing. All the girls gathered there like cups round a teapot.

That afternoon a smell of baking from the main house makes me drool and brings back memories: my fierce, resentful mother, smashing an egg into the Betty Crocker mix, the stink of burning, the apartment full of smoke. Other kids had chocolate or lemon birthday cakes. I never had one that didn't taste of charcoal.

Now I imagine Beth in her kitchen, restoring normality to her shaken world with a nice batch of brownies, with walnuts or pecans in . . . or maybe it's one of her sublime buttercream sponges, lemon or my favourite, coffee.

Warm cookies and a strawberry genoese is what we find, those of us who turn up for tea. And there's Beth, wearing a tight little smile, and then Nick, off for a stroll, pausing to praise the cake and invite her to join him.

How's it going, Glen?

Oh just fine!

. . . last year, at the retreat in Aix, they had manuscript workshops . . . – I found it *so* helpful . . . are you th...

My fellow scribes stand around figuring things out. The Hardimans are back together. Beth has triumphed, the relationship is alive and kicking. The novelists fix the couple with their scavenging eyes. Probably they would prefer the marriage to be a corpse. They can't help it, they have plots to feed. For a moment I'm tempted to share all the stuff I'd overheard, Nicholas's lies and so on, but I hold back. Eavesdropping in the toilet isn't exactly great. Really I should have coughed or made retching sounds to warn them.

The Hardimans walk far off into the field, where perhaps Nick is telling Beth the truth, who knows?

It wasn't the plan, but I allowed Nicholas back into our bed, and eventually we made love. I've always had an impulse to soothe. Afterwards I lie readjusting my image of Nadia Patel. "Born in Surrey" and "not particularly beautiful", according to Nick. So I delete the gazelle eyes, Bollywood belly and Tantric know-how I'd given her. This still leaves Nadia hot, forbidden and, now she's been spurned, perhaps more dangerous. But Nicholas has chosen me, and that's enough. It doesn't pay to go over *why* he has, even though the list is extensive:

I am dear, good, loving, kind, patient, reliable, indispensable. . .

God, why is virtue so dreary?

Our clean start has meant just a return to routine, as if nothing happened. Nick is back in the Shed with his novel. The hens lay, the geese fatten, the gardens grow, and in their rooms the writers write or dream or doze. All over Stonefield, from the compost heaps to the authors' barns, I'm aware of silent industry.

I wander around as if checking for damage, for cracks caused by our domestic tremors. But everything is reassuringly intact. I love it here. I love my husband. I shut my eyes and even after twelve years living in the country I can't help it. I'm moved almost to tears by the sounds – the rooks, bees, woodpigeons. And the smells: hay, organic compost, the herbs in my *potager*, where Andy is weeding.

What, Beth? What country smells make me nostalgic? ...well, can't say any do?

None!? Not from your childhood? Not woodsmoke? Or cows' breath?

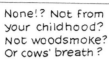 Nope

 Well...I suppose GLUE does...yeah...sniffing glue down by the war memorial when I was twelve...yeah....

Glue?

That's what we did... ..like the kids do now.. ...well, prob'ly they're doing other stuff, too - *Stuff* **we** couldn't get ....

As we're talking, the burglar alarm goes off at Winnards Farm. Very loud, on and on. My first worry is that it will disturb the writers, and when we reach the lawn, Glen, the American academic, is there, lumbering up and down, looking fed up.

What to do? Burglary is big round here and that farmhouse has been lying empty for a couple of months. Ever since the owner Mrs Drewe died.

Probably just kids

Gaad!! Don't these alarms cut out after a while?

 I'll walk over there...take a look....

Hey, hold on, Andy. Isn't it dangerous? ...like there could be bad guys over there... you know seriously ... *criminal*...

Omigosh, hey! Is that a gun in your pocket?

Gun? No... just a roll of leaflets.

Leaflets?? Oh great. That'll make 'em scared! That'll make 'em crap their pants!

I mean, are you *serious*?? C'mon, Andy...haven't you got a rifle or a fowling piece or something?

Got my dog

DDrinnnggg

I must be crazy. I should be working in my room, not going to check an activated burglar alarm. But in a macho moment I offered to go with Andy. I realise now that it was for Beth's benefit, I didn't want her thinking me a total pantyhose. Which of course I am. I'm kind of nervous of burglars, terrified of cows, even young ones. I hate thistles, I'm hot, out of breath and about to have a seizure keeping up with Andy Cobb. Fortunately he slows down when he's asked questions and stops to show me one of the leaflets he distributes round the district.

I learn three things about Andy:
• He studied design at college, had a studio set-up over in Hadditon, him and his girlfriend, until it folded and she walked out – or maybe it was the other way round.
• He learned about gardening from planting motorway verges.
• He was born on the farm where we're heading, as was his dad, his dad's dad and so on. Winnards Farm is the Cobbs' ancestral home, or it was until Andy was 14 when, as he puts it, "Everything went arse-shaped for Dad. No money in dairy unless you're big." They had to sell up. The cattle and land were bought by a consortium. The farmhouse was sold separately to Londoners, I guess sold to this Mrs Drewe who's just died. The Cobbs moved to a modern box on the edge of Hadditon.

Andy says, "Winnards was a nice old farm." Whenever Andy starts with "nice old" I've come to expect a fearsome catalogue of gross "rustic" innovations. This is true of his ancient family home: "Massive conservatory. Millstone water feature in the garden, pigs made out of wire on the lawn, stepping stones. Townie crapola."

By now we can actually see the farm, but I'm just too pooped to take much in. "You stay here with the dog", Andy says, "I'll go and take a look."

Anyone home?

CREAK CREAK THUD!

...but how should I know Mum's code? I've never set the bloody alarm!....So what is it?.... ...1981...The Royal Wedding? How the f— should I know that!?

:SNIFF:

CREAK CREAK!

So it isn't burglars who set off Mrs Drewe's alarm, it's just a girl, one of her daughters.
Andy tells me this as we go back to Stonefield – the long way round, avoiding cows, mud, etc. (My choice.)

So...she sexy, Andy... this girl?

Well, ye-ah...but I only saw her back view and it's a while since I last met her.... She's a Londoner now- she don't come here much...

Didn't she visit her mom?

I dunno. Her sister did – saw *her* around once or twice...she's the married one...she's a lawyer or something... This one's *Tamara*...she's the one who wrote about her nose job.

She had a nose job?

Yeah... you read *The Monitor*, Glen?

Nope

Nor do I...but Beth does...She was saying Tamara's got her own column....

But seems she made her name doing consumer-testing sort of thing...She did plastic surgeons...discovered a load of unqualified shysters...Got her nose done by a good'un.

But did it *need* doing, her nose?

Well, she did have a bit of a hooter.... Suited her...I quite liked it...

So I suppose she's come here to sort her mother's things...put the house on the market...flog it to some banker wanker...

Well, it's a nice house ...in a nice place...

Oh, very **NICE**!! No shop, no bus, no school, no post office, no community any more! Just a load of ponced up, over-priced real estate .....

Look at it! *Cottage Cheesecake!*

Hanging **bloody** baskets! Outsiders! *Rich* bastards!

You'd like a village of **POOR** bastards, right?...Like in olden times... shivering round dung fires...

Yeah, well they may be when the oil runs out...

The next evening we're gathered for drinks in the garden at Stonefield.

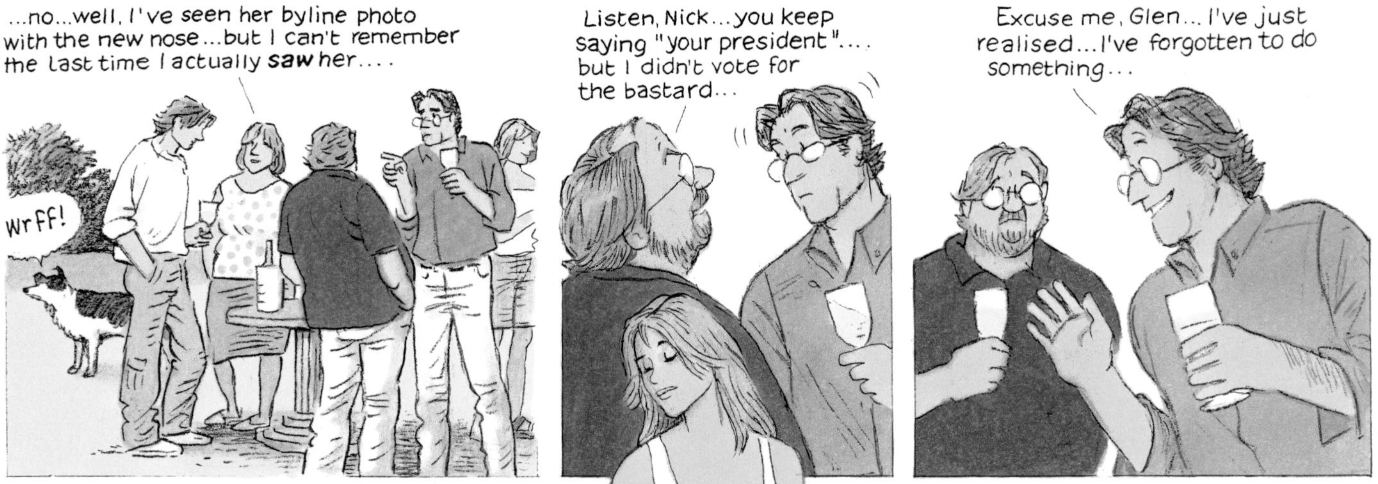
...no...well, I've seen her byline photo with the new nose...but I can't remember the last time I actually **saw** her....
Wrff!
Listen, Nick...you keep saying "your president"....but I didn't vote for the bastard...
Excuse me, Glen... I've just realised...I've forgotten to do something...

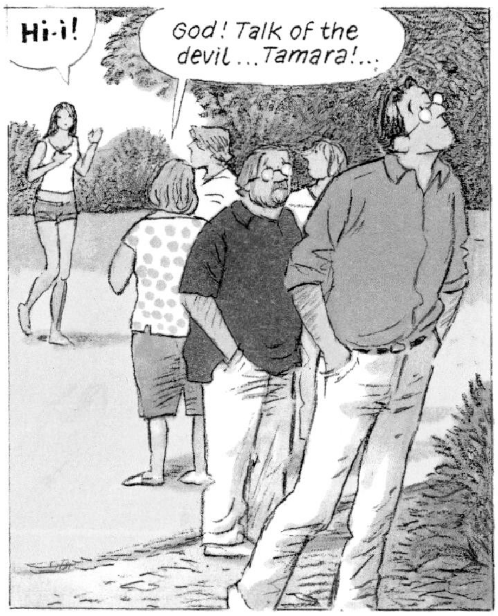
Hi-i!
God! Talk of the devil...Tamara!...

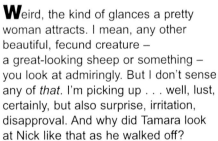

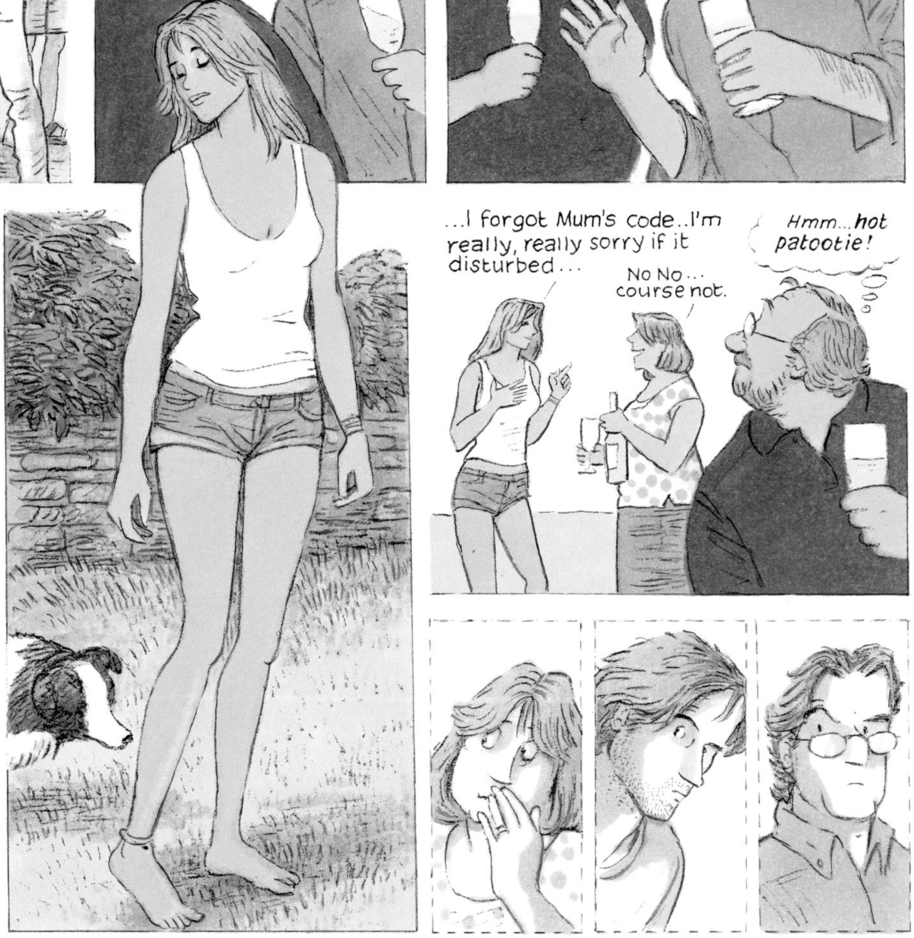
...I forgot Mum's code..I'm really, really sorry if it disturbed...
No No... course not.
Hmm...**hot** patootie!

Weird, the kind of glances a pretty woman attracts. I mean, any other beautiful, fecund creature – a great-looking sheep or something – you look at admiringly. But I don't sense any of *that*. I'm picking up . . . well, lust, certainly, but also surprise, irritation, disapproval. And why did Tamara look at Nick like that as he walked off?

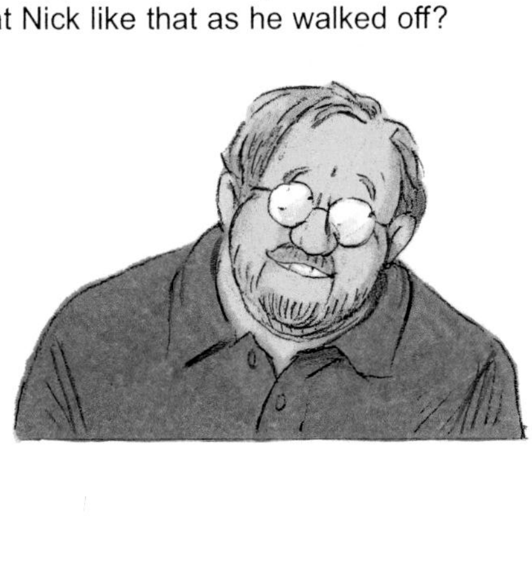

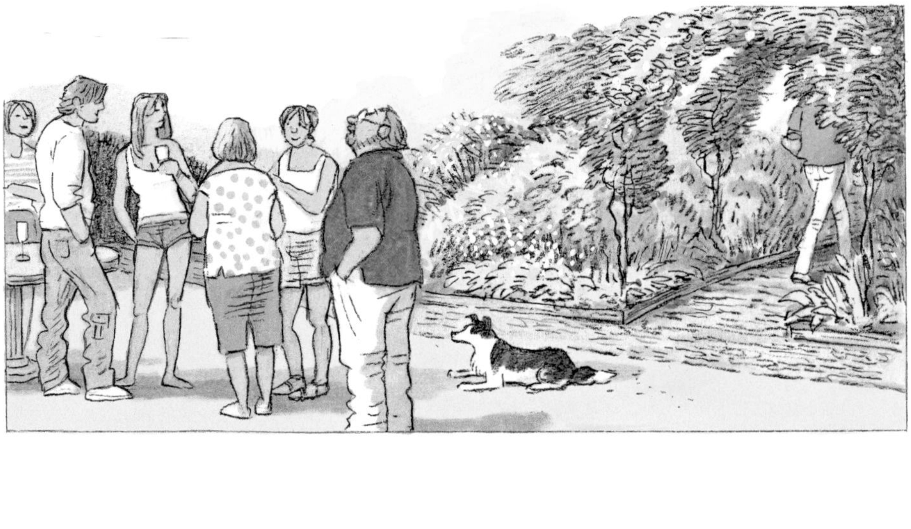

Of course I fall in love with Tamara, along with everyone else – except for Nicholas, who doesn't come back. As she moves round the gathering I watch people succumb. It's as if she's picking us off, one by one, each of us receiving the full force of her radiance, her smile, her warmth, her interest, all of it seemingly genuine and unforced. She's Princess Charming, people smile right back, they open up to her in a way they never have in a week at Stonefield. Even uptight Miranda. And Beth – I never knew Beth once worked for the BBC.

...I was a lowly researcher.... Nicholas was a guest on the programme...

That's how you met! How romantic!

...writing a series of word images...about dislocation...isolation ....

Andy!

You're a professor at *London* University?

Uh...well...at *a* London university... yes.

When my turn comes, we're almost alone, Tamara and I. Beth is long gone to the kitchen, and smells of dinner are luring others to the main house. Is it the wine that makes me blab about my ex-wife, my ex-girlfriend, about my time living in Paris, the struggles with my novel? Tamara is so intrigued. And so intriguing, I have to ask her some stuff – her boyfriend, her goal in life, and so on.

Well I'm into journalism, but I'd like to make it in fiction before I'm **35**.... Maybe do **2** or **3** novels...maybe then do a children's book...

As simple as that, eh?

And then maybe a swimwear collection...a chat show...a pasta sauce range .....yeah?

What's that supposed to mean?

Uh...nothing..nothing... just you reminded me of my students...uh...

I ought to go.

Tamara has already declined Beth's invitation to dinner. She's going to walk home across the field, the way she came. In her bare feet, for God's sake.

The way to the garden gate is gravelled. At this point I would have swept up and carried Tamara Drewe over the burning coals of Hell, let alone a garden path. If I'd had one, I'd have flung down my cloak, I feel so courtly, so gallant. For a few marvellous nano-seconds my hands grip her...

I've screwed up majorly. Princess Charming looks at me like the fat, drunk groper she thinks I am. Then she sashays off into the field. God, what a tease.

Here...let me...

Don't! Don't **touch me!!!**

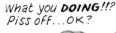

What you **DOING!!?** Piss off...OK?

Beth:

Our daughter's here for the weekend. She asks me to read through some of her dissertation on the Taliban, for whom, apparently, there's only one way of dealing with women, which is to treat them as livestock. Women must be kept confined like veal calves, with restricted access to light and fresh air. This is the only way of discouraging lewd thoughts in men. I tell Lulu about Tamara and the thoughts *she* must provoke. It was so astonishing last night to see how she'd changed. She used to be rather mousey, rather horsey, always in baggy fleeces. It was her sister Poppy who was the pretty one, more like the mother. And bright too; she went to Cambridge. Poppy was supposed to be the charmer, Tamara the difficult one. Well, not any more. Tamara charmed the pants off everyone, including me.

...I've offered to take her mother's clothes to Oxfam... well, I felt sorry...sad losing your mother....Tamara says she won't sell the house, she wants to live here....I do think her **nose** is a mistake...taken away all the character...

She never used to wear stuff like that, did she? When she was in publishing, Nick? You ran into her once or twice, didn't you — when you were with Impala Books?

Can't remember.

I found those **shorts** really irritating! Just **so** obvious!

What's irritating, Mum?

Dressing like a sex object.... Sucking up to male fantasies.

But **you** wore Hot Pants.

No, I never did, Lulu! I never went around with half my buttocks hanging out, like that....I mean, **why DO** it?

To annoy people like you...

Exactly...to be provocative...And, well there **are** consequences if you dress like that...if you look like a sex toy, you get treated like one...and you can't complain if men...well, sometimes I feel sorry for men... What **do** they do?

What they do is **deal** with it. Grow up and deal with it!

Stop making excuses for them, like they can't control themselves....Listen, Mum, I'm trying to do this Sudoku...OK?

Anyway.... wearing tight things in **this** weather...she'll get thrush... ....

Nicholas: Recollection of Tamara Drewe

...MUST BE...FIVE YEARS AGO. WHEN "DANGEROUS BENDS" CAME OUT. THE PROMOTIONAL TOUR, WEST COUNTRY LEG. TOOLING WESTWARDS, ME, THE DRIVER AND THE PUBLICITY GIRL. NOT EMMA, THE USUAL ONE – SHE WAS ILL. A SUBORDINATE STEPPED IN...TAMARA...WHO CLAIMED TO KNOW ME, SAID SHE USED TO SEE ME IN THE POST OFFICE IN EWEDOWN...HER MUM LIVED NEAR ME...AT WINNARDS FARM.....

What a coincidence!

I just want to say I'm such a fan!

very kind of you!

NICHOLAS HARDIMAN

TAMARA: NOT BAD – LOOKING, BIG NOSE, HIGHLY EFFICIENT.

Five minutes..then we must hit the road!

ROOMS HAD BEEN BOOKED AT THE TOLLHOUSE (3 STARS). DINNER AT A LOCAL ITALIAN. NOT GOOD ENOUGH FOR ME.

I'll come clean – I've had a better idea...I've booked us into **The Bay**. Much more comfortable...decent chef!

God! But that'll break the budget... um...tsk...

SAID I'D PAY THE DIFFERENCE. DINNER ON ME. MY PLEASURE. WAS SHE PLEASED?

Look, will you stop trying to get me pissed! God, you're an arsehole!

Whatever's the matter?

Just about everything! Look, I'm doing my job...

I'm not on a **DATE** with you!

I saw the look the waiter gave you...like I'm your bit of stuff! "Quiet table at the back", you said...it's just so **cheesy**!!...

I'm not a writer's perk!

Rather presumptuous of you...**you** think I fancy **you**....as a **PERK**? Really, Emma, **last thing** I think about you, can assure you of that...   ....

OK Nicholas...I'm going back to the Tollhouse...I'm knackered! I'll see you there in the morning at 10... in the lobby.

No pudding? OK...you run along then...

And my name's **Tamara**... at least you could bloody try and remember that!

Glen:

My Sunday evening stroll takes me past Andy's cottage, and I knock on the window. Andy, what does he do for fun except – judging from the smell – get stoned? I really don't get him. I know he has some on-off thing with one of the girls at The Rick, but he just seems happy being alone, green and composty, watching stuff grow.

I mean, if I was a hunky guy like Andy I'd really fancy my chances with Tamara. I'd get right in there, although if I were him I'd take a bath, change my clothes first. There's quite a pungent bouquet round Andy. Not exactly unpleasant: earth, dog, tobacco, engine oil, that kind of thing.

Hell, she's unattached, Andy! What're you waiting for? You like her, don't you?

Mn...yeah...well, I used to a bit...

But well, you know...I'm not her type...not some rich, London smart-arse...

Your trouble, Andy - you think like a **LOSER**!

Well I **AM** a **LOSER**!

I went bust...my house was re-possessed...the girlfriend left.... The reason I'm here is because the cottage goes with the job...

I'm totally dependent on the Hardimans...

But Andy, you could change all that! Get in there! Call Tamara... Play your cards right...**MARRY** her!...**Think** about it, you'd get the girl **and** to live in your ancestral home!

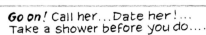
Go on! Call her...Date her!... Take a shower before you do....

So long!

Piss off, Glen!

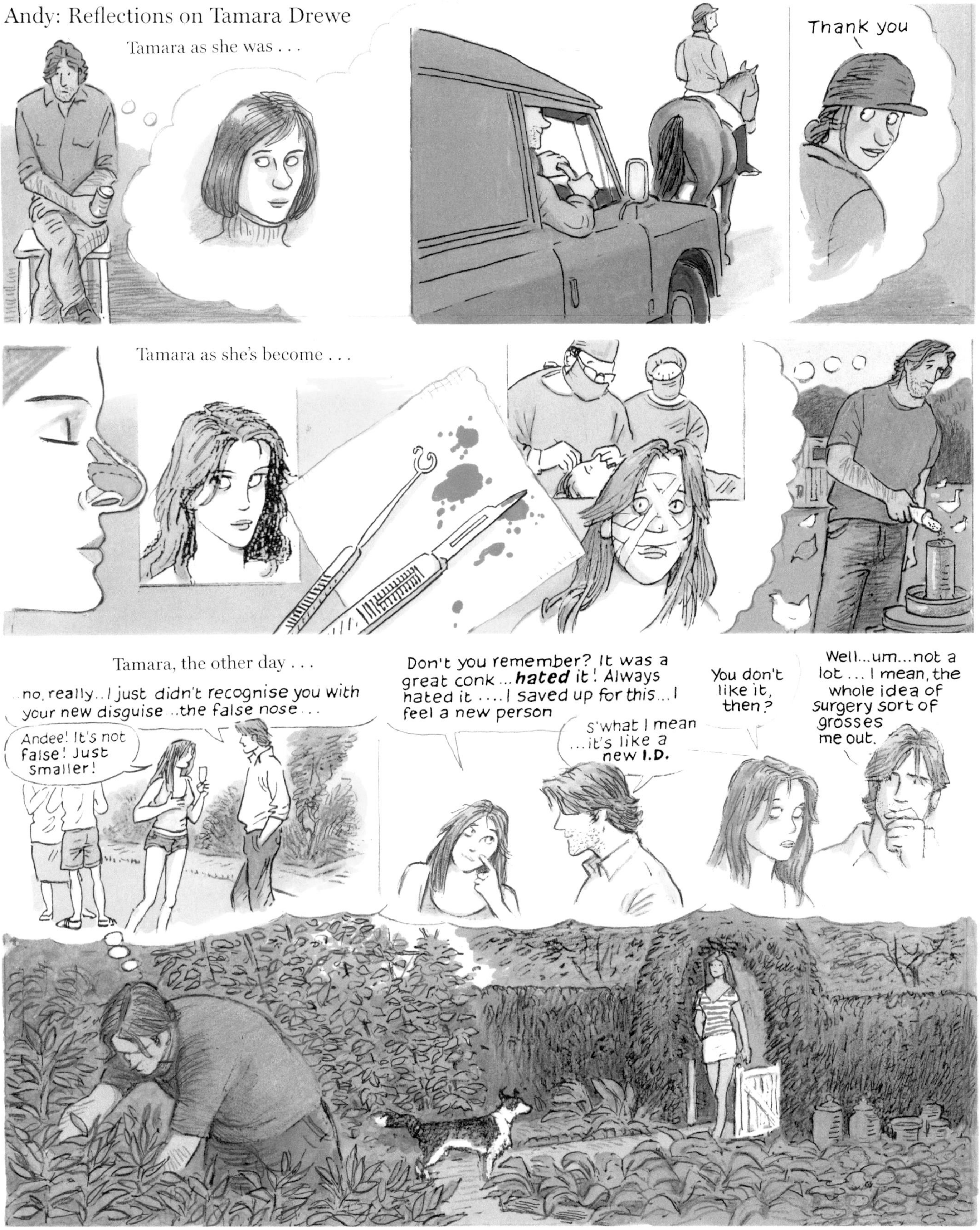
Andy: Reflections on Tamara Drewe
Tamara as she was . . .
Thank you
Tamara as she's become . . .
Tamara, the other day . . .
..no, really..I just didn't recognise you with your new disguise..the false nose . . .
Andee! It's not false! Just smaller!
Don't you remember? It was a great conk...hated it! Always hated it ....I saved up for this...I feel a new person
S'what I mean ...it's like a new I.D.
You don't like it, then?
Well...um...not a lot ... I mean, the whole idea of surgery sort of grosses me out.

See, I've always dreamed of doing this at Winnards Farmhouse...you know, a smallholding...having a proper veg garden like Beth's here...

I'd have chickens like these...maybe a goat or two... I'd be self-sufficient – and it'd give me plenty of ideas to write about...

Won't have time for much writing...and what about when you're in London?

Well that's where I hoped you'd come in, Andy...if you had time to kind of look after things....I'd pay you properly, of course...

Tsk! Oh God!

What!?

Just all this bloody myth-making about living off the land...like it's all **SO LOVELY**....Gives my arse the 'eadache! ...You'd write about being a smallholder...**I'd do the work, that it?** What a **bloody con!**

Splut!

I know who you are! Gary Pound, you ought to be shagging well shot!..and the rest of you.....catch you here again...I'll tell your mums!

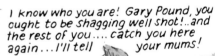

Now, **that's** what you should write about, Tamara...

...Imagine what it's like for those kids living round here..three-quarters of the village stinking rich incomers...and **their** mums stuck in Aspen Close on Benefit.....

Disgusting, this egg... there..that's better.

Anyway, Andy, you'll think about what I asked you ... won't you?

AUTUMN

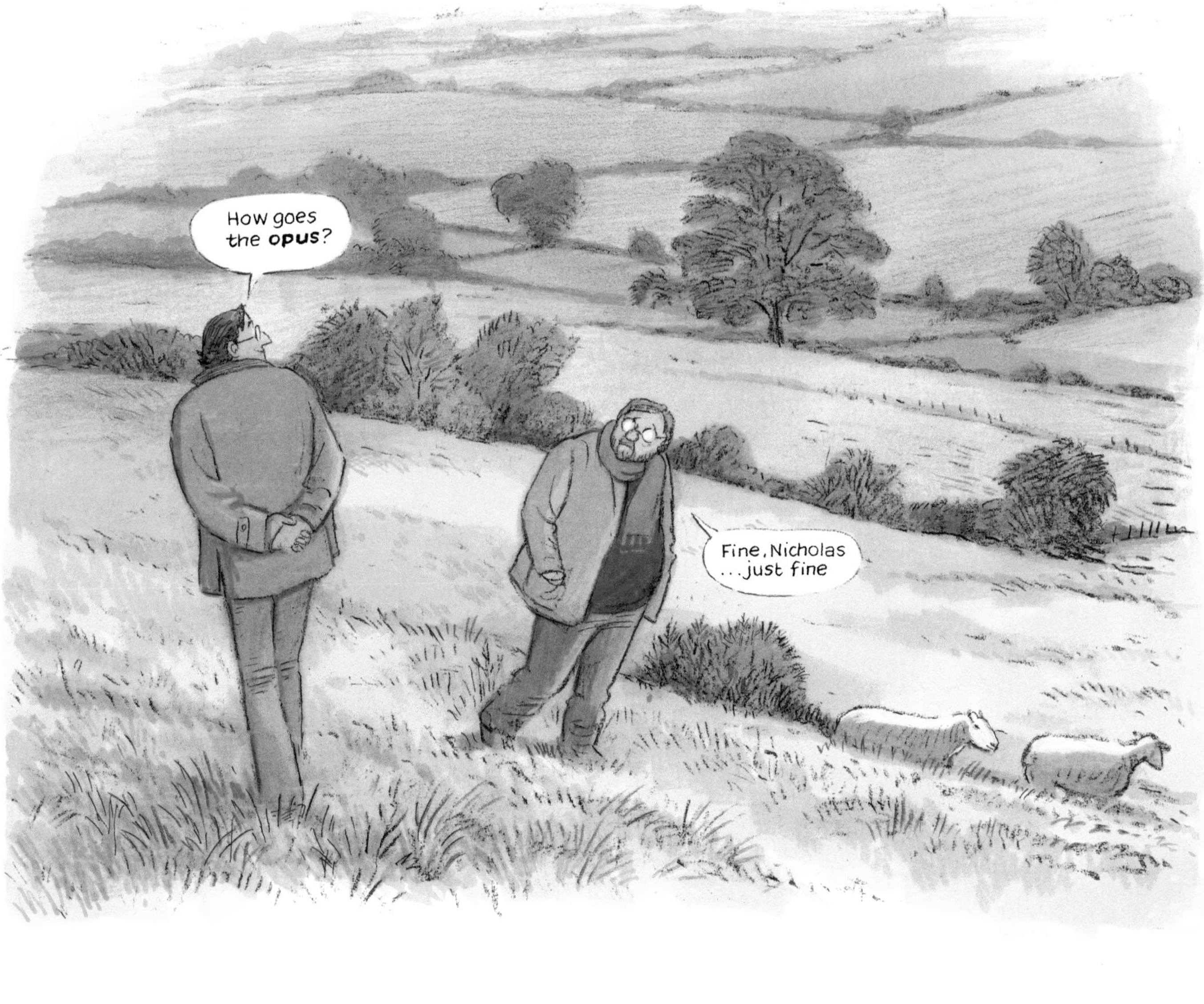
How goes the **opus**?
Fine, Nicholas ...just fine

Walking away from Nicholas, I realise I make the same sort of snidey comments to Tamara Drewe as *he* does to *me*. Like I'll ask her if she's written a film script yet. Why do I want to put her down? Why does she annoy me so much?

She's been round at Stonefield several times. I've watched her from the barn asking Beth and Andy about plants and, probably, finding out other things too. She's so damned nosy. Without meaning to, you find yourself telling her all kinds of personal stuff. I told her about breaking up with Maggie and I wish I hadn't. Not that I have huge secrets. God, if I did, I wouldn't go within 500 miles of Tamara.

It's weird talking to her. You think she's coming on to you: she aims this scorching look and you're transfixed with lust, I'm not kidding. But *she's* kidding. It's as if she has an erotic stun gun and you're just target practice. Just her bit of fun, raising the hopes of old fatsos like me. *Really* insulting, when I think about it.

The other day when I met her coming from the mailbox, she wanted the lowdown on Nicholas . . .

...you just never see him around... What's he *do* all day?

What writers like him do...perform in public...write...

Look, cut it out...you don't have to do that, you know?

Do *what*?

Make with the goo-goo eyes...fourth time around, it's a turn-off.

??

I have to tell you? OK. You fixed your nose, you look *hot*. I know it, *you* know it... the *whole world* knows it...

Is that **ALL** you want people to think about you?...It's not *that* interesting...

You might be really intelligent for all I know.

It's true, you don't see much of Nicholas Hardiman. Thankfully he keeps to his shed in the garden, a place I never go near. It's where he spends all day "pandering to popular taste," as he puts it. The times we do meet I want to kick him hard in the butt. He practically curtsies to me, like I'm Henry James. So fucking ironic, Americans don't get that stuff, do they? *Asshole.*

Take the other night. Nicholas doesn't often join us for dinner, but when there's a crime-writing weekend, he appears. He kept making these dumb statements and every time I disagreed he drowned me out with the electric carving knife. And then he talked, non-stop. Horse shit, total horse shit.

...sure you'll agree, Glen.. ...**MAD** expanding them, isn't it? **Too** many students in the universities, who'd be much better suited to vocational courses...

... I think the real secret of being a writer is learning to be a convincing liar...I mean, that's what we are: story tellers...**liars**....

Next he turned to the state of journalistic writing.

...**every** other word is "I"... and the **clichés!!**..."a girl's gotta do what a girl's gotta do" .... I ask you!

And this is typical: a glamorous by-line photo above a load of self-deprecation...about how god-awful she looks in the morning... "I need a leper's bell to warn people" ...etc,etc ...**Eurchh yuk!!**

Could you give us, p[...] few tips[...] style?

Oh, come on, Nick...it's not meant to be Shakespeare!... Everyone writes drivel at some stage...

It was Tamara's column he was trashing. (Actually I agree with him pretty much about that.) But Nicholas is a jerk. Why Beth took him back I don't know, she's so indulgent. But I guess I have to be glad she did. Without his payroll Stonefield couldn't exist, and then where would I be?

When I told folks the novel's going great, I was lying.
As agonising day followed agonising day, I panicked, and began to think of giving up. Even began to envy writers like Tamara and Nicholas. Really I did. They know their limits and write within them, no sweat.

But I have to finish this book! Apart from *amour propre*, so much depends on it: my standing at the university, and maybe my tenure too. I've published so little, and my course isn't that popular. Also I'm three years past the delivery date and, in theory, Fantail could ask for the money back – even their chicken-shit advance. Which would suck majorly.

And then, suddenly, LIGHT! I see the way to go. My book has many glittering parts but it doesn't work, like a chandelier with faulty wiring. Dismantling and repair is usually a downer, but this time is different.

It's like I've been given enormous new batteries. A constant surge of creative power carries me right through the day. I've never written like this, so clearly, so fluently, I can't stop writing. I'm in a state of writerly bliss, oblivious to everyone and everything. Sure, I check my e-mail and the letters Maggie sends on. I exercise, eat dinner, say hello, and make polite. I know I do. But nothing in this wonderful place intrudes. While I take a walk my room cleans itself, the icebox refills with beer. The dirty laundry in its bag disappears one day and returns clean the next. Outside my barn the leaves fall, days shorten, people come and go.

Andy? Where are you?

Beth:

I'm pretty sure Astrid, the younger goat, is on heat. She's bleating and tail-wagging – and, if I'm right, she really ought to be off soon to the local billy. It's an event I've been planning for. I want to ask Andy when is the right moment to take her, but where bloody is he? These days he's never here when I want him.

Andy, it's Beth. It's 4·15...where <u>are</u> you? If you're where I think you are, it's not good enough. Please ring me.

You see, Tamara Drewe is trying to poach Andy. I knew something was up when jobs in the garden were left undone: the mowing was interrupted, Andy was missing, late to start, early to go home. I have faced him with it because it's so unlike him. Andy's an open, honest sort of bloke. You know where you are with him.

...what's going on? I don't know where you are half the time....

Well, see...I agreed with Tamara I'd keep an eye on the farmhouse for her...while she's up in London...that's all.

Oh. Well, I wish I'd known.

I mean, it's fine in your own time...but not in the hours I'm paying you.

There's no sign of Andy. I really need to know when to get the blessed goat to the billy. So I drive round to Winnards Farm, and there he is out the back, double digging.

"Keeping an eye on the house", **MY FOOT!** You're making a bloody great garden!

It was hard to say no.... She...she wants a veg garden like yours...

Not at my expense she doesn't! Right now, you should be at Stonefield!

It's not like you...what the hell's got into you?

Dunno... I'm sorry...

OK, Andy, you sort out your priorities...if you want to work these sort of hours for Tamara, **FINE**...but I'd have to look for someone else...

Yuk! Does she _have_ to die like this? _Really,_ Nick! Very _nasty!!_

Fraid so.

Right...now, on page 176...if you want Rosa to be somehow alerted that Archer's been in the bathroom...what I suggest is: in the lunch scene you give them **asparagus**...later, he pees...and she picks up on the pong...OK?

That do? _Nick?_ You listening?

Nick is frowning at Tamara Drewe, who's out in the yard, gazing at her reflection in a CD. She's strutted about for the last ten minutes, showing everyone she's here. I'd invite her in for coffee, but Nick's adamant he doesn't want any distraction. "What's she hanging about for?" he asks. For Andy and the goat, that's what. Tamara's invited herself to Astrid's nuptials, and I can't say I'm pleased – goats don't like strangers around at such times. Andy assured me Tamara would keep in the background, so I said OK, because ever since I told Andy off I'm feeling rather bad about him.

It wasn't only to do with his timekeeping. If I'm honest, it's jealousy. I mind him working for Tamara for proprietorial reasons. It was me who offered him a job and put him back on his feet. Without me he'd still be drinking and wallowing in his bad luck. Still, I don't own him and I can't blame him for setting his sights on Tamara, if that's the plan, to cosy up with the girl who now owns his family home. Why wouldn't he want to cultivate her garden, get his feet under the table?

Of course, it may be just that – _gardening_, and I'm reading things into it. Tamara has another life in London and probably much more exciting things to do than go in Andy's smelly Landrover with a goat.

I thought it would be terrific material to write about...

Just don't think of going near the billy...

see, they pee on their beards and things - you never get rid of the smell!

Here's the bride...

..May be a wasted journey, Tamara

You never can tell...

If she's ready, she'll stand for him...if not, she won't...

We're off, then Beth.

Don't forget the paperwork... Drive carefully

She come on this time yesterday...

That should do

Lovely job

I stink: therefore I am...that's old Darcy's motto...now, he's as good as gold...

..Yeah, it's a stimulus...olfactory stimulus...some of it's pee, some of it's from a scent gland on his head...

So how long does her heat last?

Oh about 36 hours

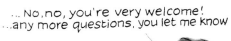

Don't use flash...you'll put 'em off...

I'm not!

That was pretty quick

...No, no, you're very welcome! ...any more questions, you let me know

That's really nice of you!

AWAY FROM IT ALL

by **Tamara Drewe**

Last week I watched a couple meet on a blind date. He was called Darcy, satanic-looking, hairy and indescribably smelly. Her name was Astrid, She was pale, nervous and very eager.

Within seconds of meeting, they were up and at it.

And here I draw a veil and reveal that the dirty dancing was between two loved-up goats. Astrid belongs to my neighbour and Darcy is the local stud billy, whose stench at this times of year is all pervading, and as I found later, it clings particularly to clothing.

Darcy's owner, Nell Potter, says that male goats are a damn nuisance to keep, but she prefers them rather than artificial insemination. "It would be a shame to deprive the females of the courtship ritual", she says.

Nell runs Hays Farm. "Not the kind of life I'd wish on anyone, what that the farm shop isn't

God! The goats've really given you ideas!

Oh forget it...

Oh, **listen** Andy, I didn't mean to be... I'm sorry... OK? I'm sorry...

No, forget it... really.... dunno why I said it... it's balls... forget it...

Oh. You didn't mean it?

Tamara, I meant it... but I shouldn't've said it....And.....

And?

Well...without going into all the ins and outs of the cat's behind...I always felt that way about you...even **now**, with your stupid nose job.

No, don't say anything! Now...we got to get the goat home...drop you off home too... And you still want me to go ahead with your garden? Only there's your composting...your edging stuff to think of...you want raised beds or what?

BrMM!

Andy...I don't know what to say...I mean, I think you're...

Andy, I want more than anything for you to do the garden...

OK..so I'm going to London tonight.... Be back on Tuesday...

Ah

I'll see you then, promise

Bye!

Komodobar, London

It's him!...

Ben Sergeant, ex-drummer of Swipe, co-wrote Rush of Blood and Top Shelf albums; ex-partner of vocalist Fran Redford.

Hallo... Who are we?

Tamara

LOW-DOWN DOWNLOAD

Craig gets 1-2-1 with Swipe's bassist Steve Culley

Q: I hear the main reason Ben Sergeant left Swipe was because you and Fran became an item?
A: That's what he puts around and it's bollocks. Real story is his drumming got really crap. He was playing loose, flamming all the time. We just couldn't go on like that.
Q: Is it true you and Ben still aren't speaking?
A. Yeah, guess he's pretty hacked off.
Q: He introduced Fran to the band when she was nobody, right? And they'd been together like ages.
A. People move on. It just happened, her and me. I know it's tough. Life's a shit sandwich sometimes.
Q: The band owes a lot to Ben's writing talent, right?
A. Yeah, totally agree, he wrote some really balls-out stuff. I wish him we

Wouldn't print your name.... *promise!*

S'only for my stupid column ...nothing **DEEP**...just think it'd be interesting...you could shed some light on...

Why would I want to? *Hate* bloody journalists!

Oh here you are, Tamara!

We thought you'd fallen in the loo...anyway, we're off...you OK for getting home?

Yeah, fine

Cheers, Cate.

AWAY FROM IT ALL

by **Tamara Drewe**

What's it like to turn your back on fame?

I asked Dave (not his real name), an ex-member of a stellar indie rock band, who did just that. One day, unable to face another tour bus, gig, or minute of fan frenzy, he jacked it in and walked out on the band.

"Best thing I ever did," said Dave. "I got my life back." Whenever someone tells me they've "got their life back" I always ask, "And what life would that be..." ...know what this me... ...tching up on sh... ...rs, seeing you... ...rible telly and... ...h a massive... ...ing... ...the... ...fa... ...se...

So where's your boyfriend tonight?

Haven't got one... ...we split up a while ago...

And why was that?

Oh..been together since college...sort of grew out of him....he wanted to settle down ...I wanted...well...I want to **DO** something...

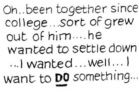

Like writing a crappy newspaper column?

NO! something *better*

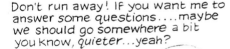

Don't run away! If you want me to answer some questions....maybe we should go somewhere a bit you know, quieter...yeah?

Mn... OK

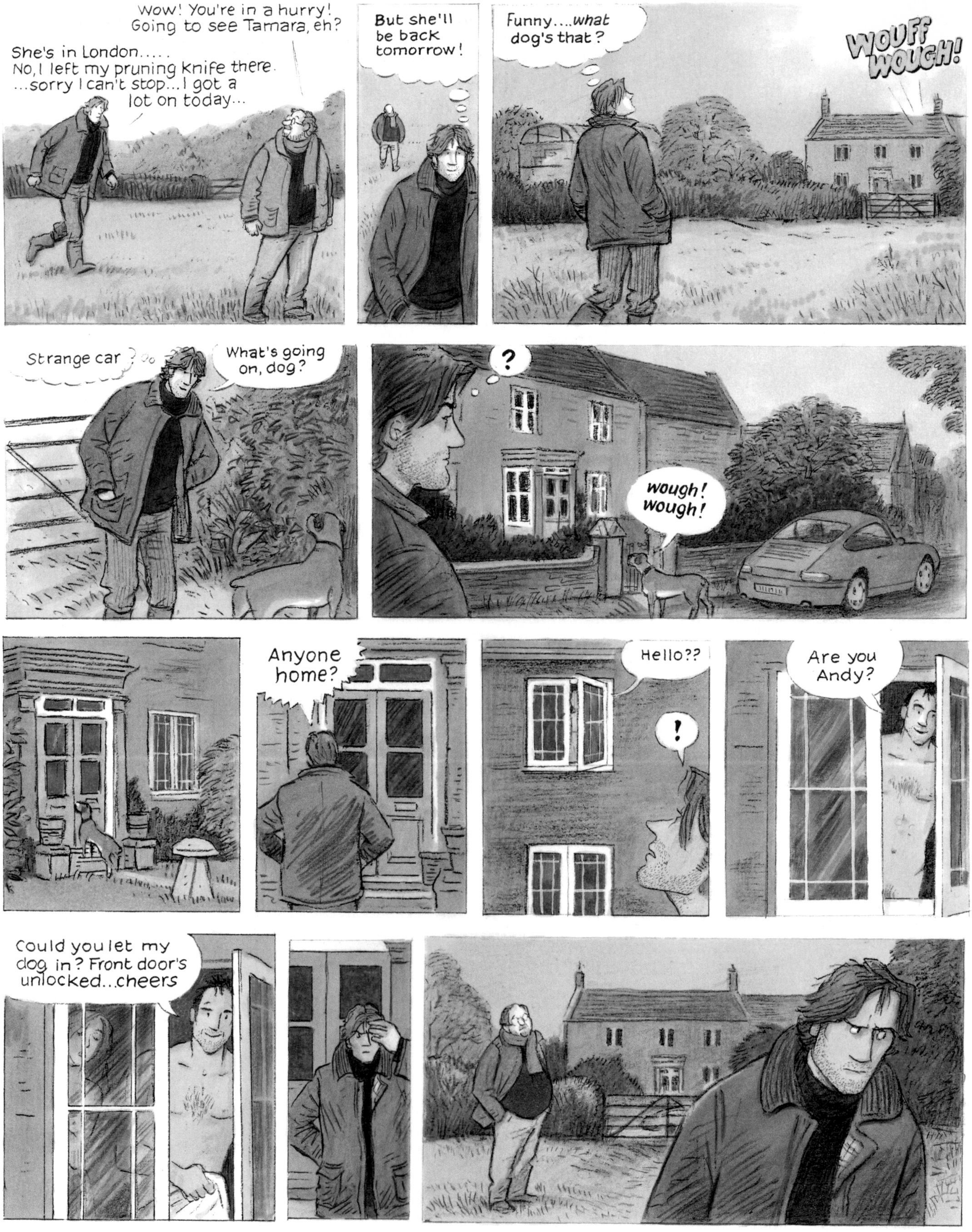
Wow! You're in a hurry! Going to see Tamara, eh?
She's in London..... No, I left my pruning knife there. ...sorry I can't stop... I got a lot on today...
But she'll be back tomorrow!
Funny....what dog's that?
WOUFF WOUGH!
Strange car?
What's going on, dog?
?
wough! wough!
Anyone home?
Hello??
!
Are you Andy?
Could you let my dog in? Front door's unlocked...cheers

Beth:

I could tell Andy was upset this morning. I asked him if he was OK, and he came out with it – Tamara's bloke, a dog, a yellow car. But with no self-pity. Yes, he did like Tamara, but he'd made a big mistake telling her, he said. Personally, I think Andy's had a lucky escape.

I'm in the office doing the e-mails when Nicholas texts three ominous words from the Shed: "COWS DOG PENNY."

We don't keep cows ourselves, but we lease our three fields to a neighbour, Penny Upmaster. She needs the extra grazing for her Belted Galloways – an arrangement I've come to regret. I used to love the idea of seeing cows from the house. They add something to the view, I've always liked pictures called "Landscape with Cattle." But now I'd almost prefer to have a phone mast in the field. Hard to say which is worse, Penny or the cows. Both are bad tempered and stare at you. The cows ruin the hedges and make a bog by the gates, but at least they don't pretend to be landed gentry.

"COWS DOG PENNY." I hear all three bellowing, barking and shouting as I hurry out of the house.

I find the cattle bunched and bawling on the far side of the field, the dog collared with baling twine and Penny berating my husband.

Nicholas! I know you're in there!

Really! Your bloody husband! Didn't lift a bloody finger to help!

He must've been watching this dog worry my cattle! Did he call it off? Did he ring me? Did he shift his arse?! *Lucky* I was passing!!

'Fraid he never notices anything when he's writing. He was probably hard at it...Working.

Oh, is that what he calls it— staring out of the window? *Tsk! Really!*

Look, all these girls could've *aborted!*

Oh calm down! It's not *our* fault...not *our* dog!

That's not the point...it's about neighbourliness! Beats me why you people want to live in the country, when you don't give a stuff about it ....Nicholas could *sit* and stare just as well in London...

What could I do, Penny? *How* nice to see you!

Oh... Nicholas

Terrific coat! You look *wonderful* in it...suits you!

What? This old thing?

Now...you, dog..... didn't Andy say something about a dog?...at Tamara's..? ....where's my phone...?

...It's Beth Hardiman...Sorry, have I disturbed you?..... It's about a dog...a *BOXER*..? Oh, good...thought it might be ...well, I've got him here...he's been chasing cows...d'you think someone could collect him?....

****

Tamara's boyfriend leaves skid marks on the gravel and releases a thunking blast of rock from the car window.

*Ooh, God! could you shush it please!? ...there're **writers** here...trying to write!*

CHUNKA TUNK!

He arrives just as I'm coming in from collecting Nick's work for the day. (Four sides of A4 – almost a chapter, written as usual in 2B pencil.) Normally I'd go straight to the study and begin putting it on the computer. But here is Ben – the name he mumbles – come to collect his errant dog. I ask him to wait while I put the precious pages somewhere safe and he smiles a slow and disarming smile which, when I think about it later, is actually rather sinister. I admit that it's probably the smile that makes me ask him into the house, where he declines tea and a piece of my lemon cake. I leave Ben in the kitchen, only to find him a minute or two later prowling round what we call the Reading Room, where our authors gather for workshops, discussions, etc. "Nosy bugger", I think.

But I quite enjoy showing people what we've done here, and he doesn't seem to be in any hurry. I give him a brief tour of downstairs, and on the way to the stables where his dog is, I show him barns, veg garden, goats, geese, my new Buff Orpingtons and so on.

...so we're totally organic and pretty well self-sufficient

*Now, **HE** is a...fairly well-known poet...if he's wearing the hat, it's a sign not to talk to him.*

Nicholas is too busy peering into the car and so is obliged to meet Ben, something I know he wanted to avoid. Nick has a thing about celebrities. That is, people richer and more famous than he is. Is Ben rich and famous? I can't say I'd ever heard of Swipe before Andy told me. It seems Ben was quite famous when he was in the band; less so now he's left it. As for rich, Andy says he must have made a bundle because he wrote all their best songs.

Nicholas Hardiman... hallo!

I know. Tamara told me about you...

Oh, really?

That's a very **un-green** car of yours...well, it's yellow, that's why! *ha ha!* Got a lot of poke I dare say

Now, we better find your dog.

As we walk to the stable suspicion begins to hatch like a maggot. It was Ben's tone. What the hell's Tamara told him about Nicholas? It didn't sound like, "You know, the writer Nicholas Hardiman lives across the field." It sounded much more loaded. And didn't Nicholas blush slightly? Oh God, not him and Tamara . . .

God!

Why's he on a ★★★★ing chain!?

WUH!

well, he was a bit out of control!

How'd you like to be ★★★★ing chained up?

Look, d'you mind showing a bit of gratitude?...We took your dog in...

You don't seem to understand...he was chasing livestock...next time he does that, he may not be so lucky... Someone'll shoot him.

Oh yeah? Someone does that, I'll ★★★★ing shoot them...

Cheers!

As soon as Ben drove off and without my saying *anything*, Nick erupted. "You can stop looking at me like that. I know what you're thinking. Just lay off!" He really lost it, swore there'd never been anything between him and Tamara, that he barely knew her, that he didn't know what Ben was insinuating and when would I start trusting him and stop behaving like the effing Stasi?

That's a bit rich. If I've become the moral police, it's Nicholas's fault. Does he think I've liked it, all these years, being his confessor, being made to feel a dreary old prude? We've always had an open sort of marriage. Affairs are OK, up to a point. Lying about them is not. Which sounds sensible and realistic, but in practice Nicholas needs the flings and I don't. He always admits them – in so many words – and I absolve him.

I just hate it. The time and energy I've wasted feeling sick about his goings on.

And that's the trouble, according to Nick – it's my suspicious mind.
After the Nadia episode he said
he thought we'd drawn a line and
moved on . . .

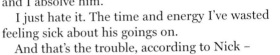

... or have we got to go through this about *every single* woman I meet? ...It's madness, Beth...

: SIGH :
I know...

The 27th? Oh, he'll be very disappointed...I know he'd love to talk to your reading group...but sadly, he's got another commitment...

...the 27th?...and who else is on the programme?...*Ah*... Yes, well I'm sure he'd like to take part...

FROM NICHOLAS HARDIMAN · STONEFIELD HOUSE · EW

Dear Ms Farr

I enclose two signed copies of my book
Famine Relief Auction as requested. Tha.

FROM NICHOLAS HARDIMAN · STONEFIELD HOUSE · EWEDOWN · BO7 9LJ

Dear Mr Stringer

Thank you for your long letter and m/s, which I am returning separately, and for your kind remarks about the most recent "Doctor Inchcombe" book. I enjoyed reading your verse drama but regret that I am, alas, not in a position to recommend a suitable publisher. You might find the Writers and Publishers Yearbook helpful. With good luck and best wishes,
Yours sincerely
Nicholas Hardiman

So..what did you make of Stonefield?

Disgusting... made you want to puke

Like your mum's stuff here...everything covered in ****ing flowers...... ****ing floral pelmets... ...really gross!

No, no...I meant the Hardimans

Them? Tossers...middle-class middle-aged...**SMUG!** – I mean, wotsername, Beth...

"Oh mai Buff Orpingtons! O, I'm saving the planet with mai organic leeks! O, I'm so self-sufficient! O, we're living off the land!"

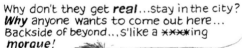

Boll-ocks!

Living off the wad her old man makes, more like!

Uhh!..that sort of **holy hush** there! "Ssh! the **WRITERS!**" she goes...like she's got ****ing **Shakespeare** staying!...... when it's only a load of ****ing nobodies in elasticated waistbands!

Oh, sometimes they've had quite good authors there – I saw the visitors' book.

You amaze me...

Why don't they get **real**...stay in the city? **Why** anyone wants to come out here... Backside of beyond..,s'like a ****ing **morgue!**

Is it?

As for him..as for your famous boyfriend Nicholarse.... What a wanker!

He's **not** my boyfriend!

Well, he tried it on, didn't he?

TRIED...once. Long time ago

Think he's avoiding me now!

So, how far **did** he get?...you didn't say....

Nowhere

Ever tries it again...I'll give him a good kicking in the slats....I'll kill him!

Beth:

The next time I run into Tamara is about three weeks later in Hadditon. I'm doing the Saturday shop with Glen, who needed a break from writing. Tamara beamed at me but ignored Glen. Because he was rude to her, he says. He thinks she's flaky and he just can't take the wraparound smiles. I think she's someone who's rather insecure, who needs constantly to reassure herself.

Oh Tamara! How're you?

I'm good

Ten minutes later I spot Tamara again, in the act of being thoroughly reassured. Heads turn, people stare, as she and the boyfriend make almost regal progress down Sheep Street. Tamara, her hand in the back pocket of Ben's trousers, smiles dreamily, as well she might. Life must be so satisfying. She's got the lot: improved looks, rich lover, good job, nice house, even celebrity of a kind.

My daughter says that Tamara is sometimes mentioned on gossip pages, but only because she's Ben's girlfriend, his appendage, in Lulu's opinion. But isn't it the other way round? Ben completes Tamara's image.

I'm still in the queue at Midi when I see Tamara for the third time. She'd left some olives on the counter.

Oh, Beth..did I tell you my news?

No...?

Ben and I are getting married! I'm so happy!

Oh how... wonderful! Congratulations!

AWAY FROM IT ALL

by **Tamara Drewe**

Sometimes you just can't win. Last week's report of the statistics on divorce in Britain makes uncomfortable reading, especially to one who's about to tie the knot.

Yes, I'm thinking of getting married, after years of staying resolutely single. The reaction in some quarters has been "About time too!" But I'm rather proud to have stayed on the shelf till now. After all, haven't I got through my twenties without (a) committing myself to someone I now loathe and (b) adding to those divorce statistics?

I share Tamara's news with Nicholas, but as any reference to her bores him to death and he has to be reminded who Ben is, and generally couldn't care less, I give up. Obviously deep in his book. As is Glen Larson, but at least he reacted. He doesn't give the marriage, if it happens, six months. I'd give it longer. Something about the way Ben and Tamara are all over each other.

Was there an engagement ring? I didn't notice. But there are certainly celebrations to mark the occasion – parties, two weekends running at Winnards Farm. Thudding music, the lane clogged with cars (not one of them with a child seat), and a gang of 30-year olds throwing frisbees in the field, a strangely depressing sight. In fact, whenever Tamara and Ben are in residence there's disturbance of one kind or another. All this screeching from the old bus shelter, you can hear it from the house. According to Andy the local kids hang out there, hoping to catch sight of Ben.

There's also something depressing when things are quiet. You'll see the curtains are drawn or the bedroom light is on mid-afternoon and you know what's going on up there. The other day when I was coming home from the post box – I always do a circuit, the outward part on the road and home over the field – I saw poor Andy in the lane. He'd just finished work in Tamara's garden . . .

When I passed I looked up at Tamara's bedroom window too. Then I walked home towards the various lighted windows of Stonefield, Nicholas a monkish figure in The Shed, bent over his next chapter.

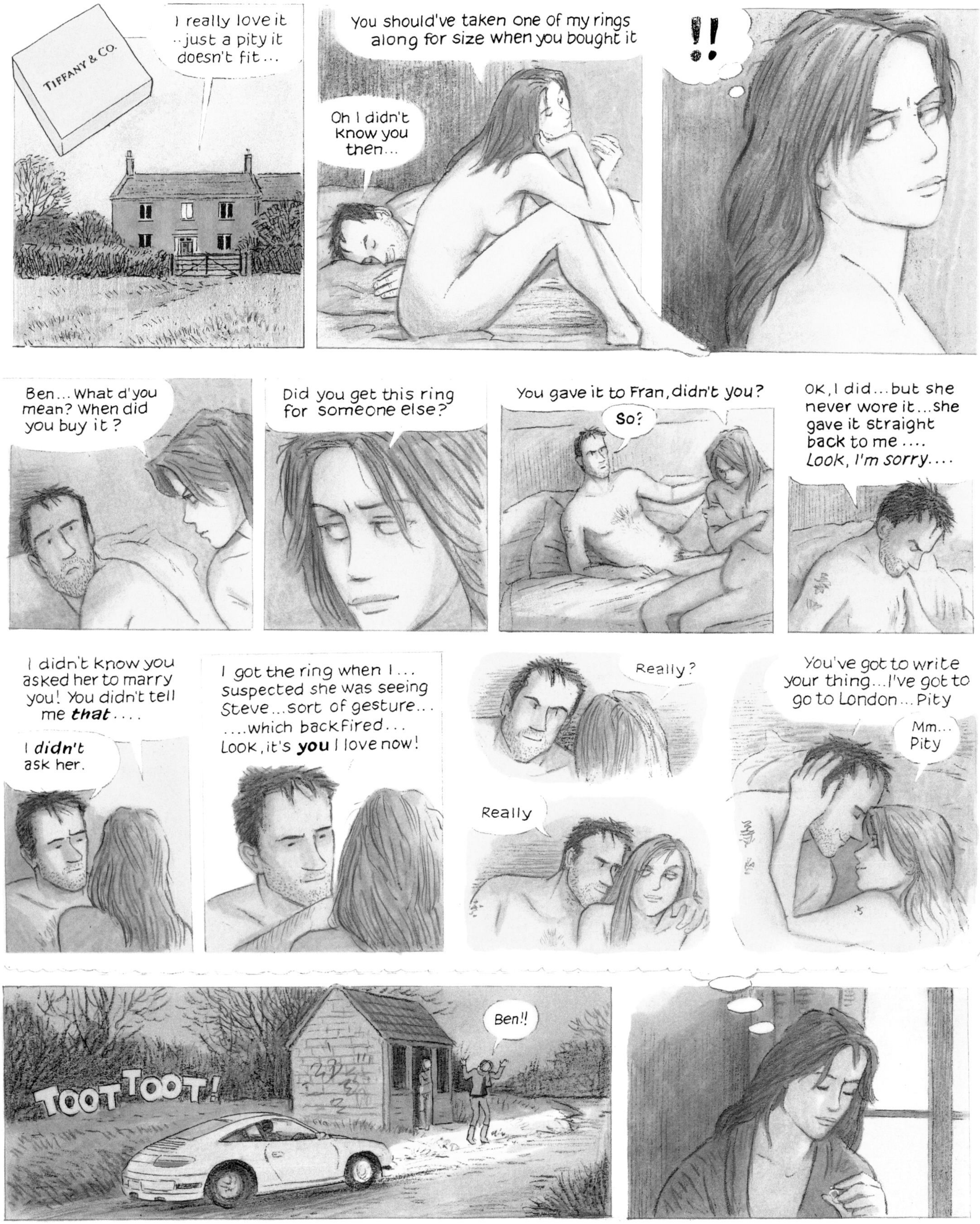
TIFFANY & CO.
I really love it ..just a pity it doesn't fit...
You should've taken one of my rings along for size when you bought it
Oh I didn't know you then...
!!
Ben... What d'you mean? When did you buy it?
Did you get this ring for someone else?
You gave it to Fran, didn't you?
So?
OK, I did... but she never wore it... she gave it straight back to me.... *Look, I'm sorry....*
I didn't know you asked her to marry you! You didn't tell me ***that*....**
I ***didn't*** ask her.
I got the ring when I... suspected she was seeing Steve... sort of gesture... ....which backfired... Look, it's **you** I love now!
Really?
Really
You've got to write your thing... I've got to go to London... Pity
Mm... Pity
TOOT TOOT!
Ben!!

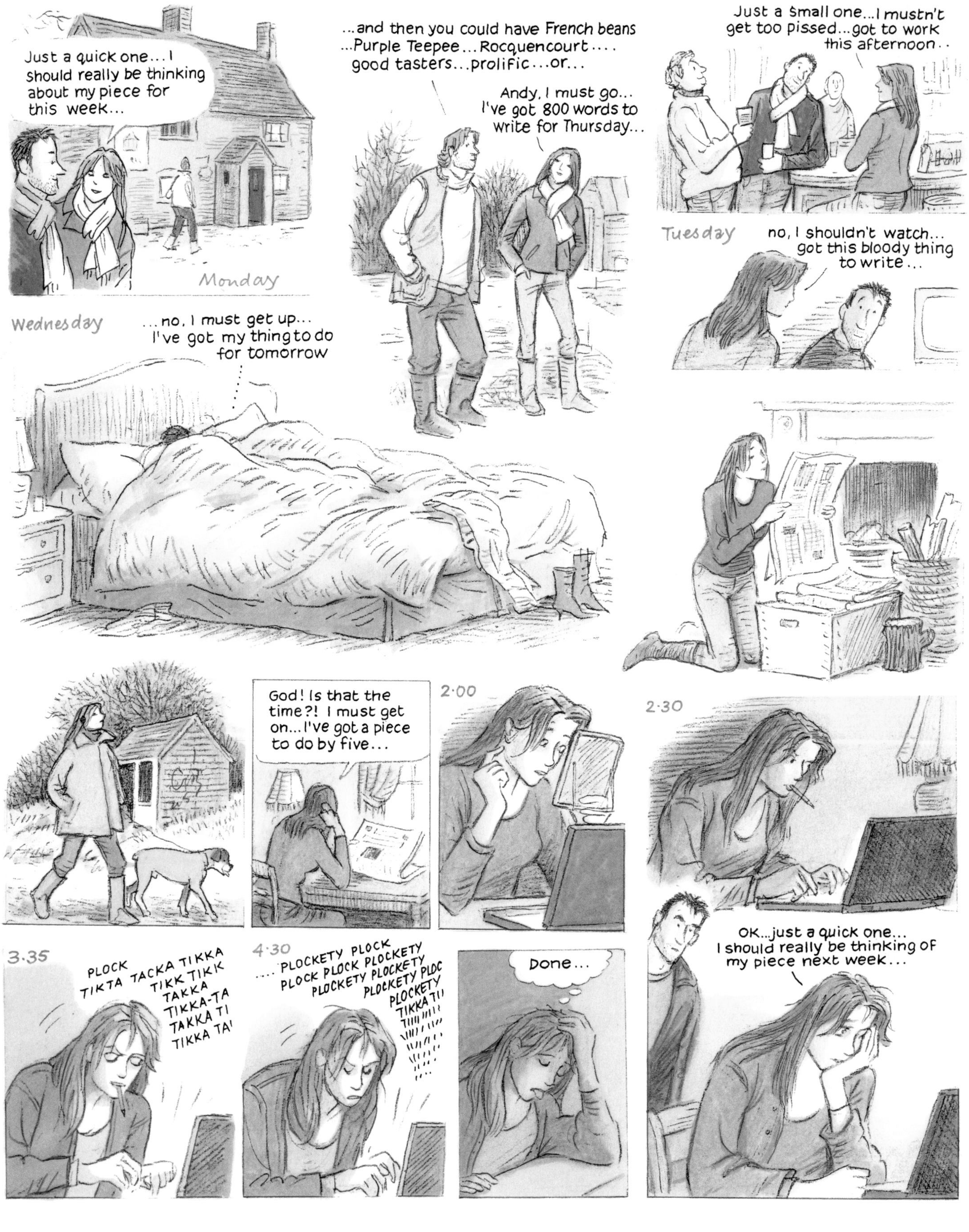
Just a quick one... I should really be thinking about my piece for this week...
Monday
...and then you could have French beans ...Purple Teepee... Rocquencourt.... good tasters...prolific...or...
Andy, I must go... I've got 800 words to write for Thursday...
Just a small one...I mustn't get too pissed...got to work this afternoon..
Tuesday
no, I shouldn't watch... got this bloody thing to write...
Wednesday
...no, I must get up... I've got my thing to do for tomorrow
God! Is that the time?! I must get on...I've got a piece to do by five...
2·00
2·30
3·35
PLOCK TIKTA TACKA TIKKA TIKK TIKK TAKKA TIKKA-TA TAKKA TI TIKKA TA!
4·30
....PLOCKETY PLOCK PLOCK PLOCK PLOCKETY PLOCKETY PLOCKETY PLOCKETY PLOC PLOCKETY TIKKA T!!
Done...
OK...just a quick one... I should really be thinking of my piece next week...

Ooh! Eight pages—not a bad day, Nick....now, one or two messages...

Your editor rang...wanted to know how you're doing...she said she's very excited... ....

...and wondered if you had a delivery date in mind—*not* that she wants you to rush things. .....What d'you want me to say? Easter-ish?

Mm

Tamara Drewe rang wanting a short interview for her column...."Your Working Day," or something *very* boring... ...I gave her a **NO**, ...that was right, wasn't it?

Yes!

And a few e-mails... Someone wants you to talk at a festival. I'll put them here... Now, you'll come in soon, won't you?

Oh God....

Beth:

I tried to talk Nicholas out of doing this signing. Yes, I do support the small bookseller, but Chris is *never* grateful, and Nick has been looking really tired. Thank God our break is coming up. We always shut Stonefield between Christmas and February and take a holiday – that is, if Nick can tear himself away from his book.

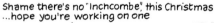

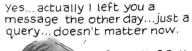

I've seen Nick do this before. He's brilliant at charming women, and equally good at snubbing them. Especially women like Tamara who think they're God's gift. I can't help looking at other reasons for Nick's standoffishness: the row about her the other day or the ghastly interview Tamara wanted to inflict on him. Of course, brusque in public can mean intimate in private . . . Oh, I must stop this! Nick loves me and Tamara loves Ben, who's sulking by the door.

Glen is telling me about the huge progress he's made with his book and the glowing report some don at Bristol gave the first five chapters; how he needs one big push to finish the thing and will I reserve the same room for him when he comes back in February? Over his shoulder I watch Ben watching Tamara work the room, and think how well I know his feelings. All the stupid evenings I've spent on the edge of a crowd checking Nick. Imagining things.

...well **WHERE** do you want to be, then? Thought you hated London
Just not **here** all the time ...so bloody boring!
!
...been thinking...maybe we could just go with the flow a bit...leave the dog with my Dad...go to L.A...
Speak to me, Ben...what d'you want to do?
Dunno
Look, I dunno! I've done everything...done everything I ever wanted to do...made money, two good albums...been papped in the press...I dunno what I want....
What about my column?! My writing...I want to do something ***more***...a book....a...
You can write anywhere...
No, I can't...anyway I can't just leave this house!
Let it...sell it...buy something better later on...France or somewhere...
But it's my home! I grew up here..!
Well, that's part of the trouble, Tamara...maybe Memory Lane for you... ...but, tell you, it ****ing does my head in...
...And **WHY** is it... whenever I look out, I see Andy's arse?
What's he **DOING**?? Why's he **HERE**? ****ing freezing out there!
Tidying up ...making the compost bays
I reckon **you're** the reason he hangs around here...I seen the way he looks at you...you like that, don't you?...people looking at you....

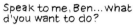

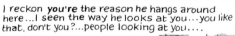

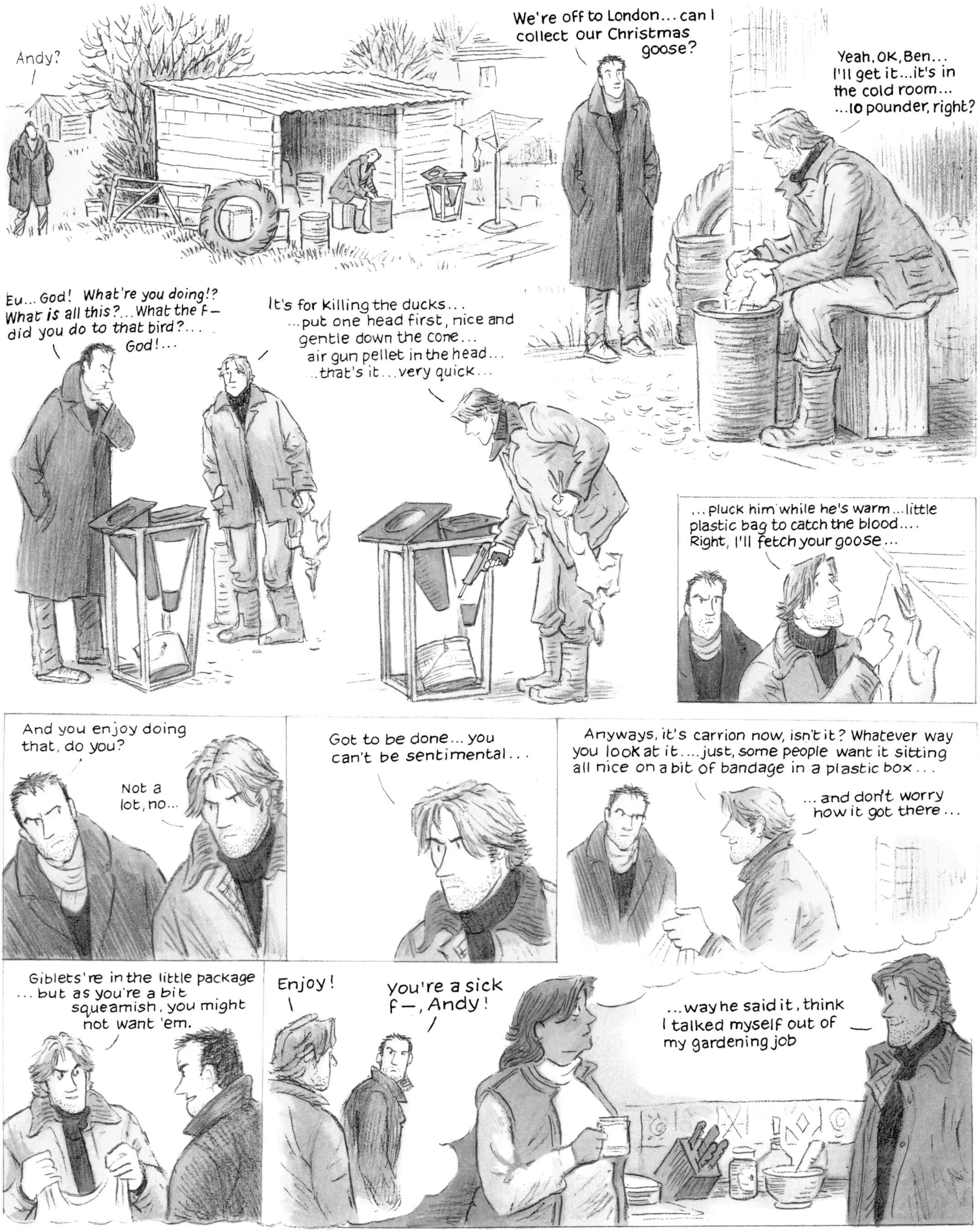
Andy?
We're off to London... can I collect our Christmas goose?
Yeah, OK, Ben... I'll get it... it's in the cold room... ...10 pounder, right?
Eu... God! What're you doing!? What *is* all this?... What the f— did you do to that bird?... God!...
It's for killing the ducks... ...put one head first, nice and gentle down the cone... air gun pellet in the head... ...that's it... very quick...
... pluck him while he's warm... little plastic bag to catch the blood.... Right, I'll fetch your goose...
And you enjoy doing that, do you?
Not a lot, no...
Got to be done... you can't be sentimental...
Anyways, it's carrion now, isn't it? Whatever way you look at it.... just, some people want it sitting all nice on a bit of bandage in a plastic box...
... and don't worry how it got there...
Giblets're in the little package ... but as you're a bit squeamish, you might not want 'em.
Enjoy!
You're a sick f—, Andy!
...way he said it, think I talked myself out of my gardening job

WINTER

Casey Shaw   Jody Long

The first time we did it is just before Christmas. Jody's idea, like most things are.

We were going to get a lift into Hadditon with Jody's mum, but decide not to – we're skint, it's freezing, and getting back means staying there bloody hours till her mum finishes her shift at Tesco.

So we go to the old bus shelter. Usually we hang around here, Ben-watching. Jody's got this super-sized crush on him, which is like totally mad. I ask you, what would Ben see in her? He's loads older, massively rich, etc., plus he lives with Tamara. We call her Plastic Fantastic because she could almost be a model. Anyway they're not at Winnards Farm. We know because we had three minutes' excitement the day before, watching them load their cars. When they passed us in the lane she blanked us, but Ben gave Jody one of his Special Looks (so she says).

Suppose we just go home...

Hey...we could go and check out round at Ryan's....he **did** ask you out...why didn't you text him back?

Why would I want to go out with Ryan?

Cheeseburger and a freezing snog... ...him telling the whole school he shagged me...**no thanks**!

I quite fancy him

You can have him

Right, Casey..we're going to Winnards Farm! ...come on!

Wot?

Why?

But... Jody!

Come on!

Look, you heard them! They're away till after New Year...they don't put the alarm on...they keep a key round the back for Andy Cobb...and I know **where**...

But Jody...what're you going to **DO**?!!

I just want to look at Ben's things... Just **LOOK**, OK?

If you're too chicken, Casey ...go home!

The first time we get into Winnards Farm we do just look at things.
OK, we have to touch some stuff to look at it, but we keep our gloves on.
All the time I want to leave, but Jody is upstairs, all over the place, looking for things of Ben's. It's sort of pervy being in their bedroom, although Jody's such a sexpert (I don't think), she says they do it everywhere, specially on the washing machine. She goes really mental when she finds this T-shirt of Ben's in the dirty clothes basket.

That's what she takes from the farmhouse the second time we do it, which is on Boxing Day afternoon. I don't want to go there, but anything's better than staying home listening to my mother having a go at my brother and my stepdad farting into the settee. This time we look at Tamara's cupboard because she's got some really cool stuff shoved away. Loads of shoes, belts, bags, etc. all jumbled together like they're a load of rubbish. Real designer stuff, no question.
Jody hands me this Chloë bag, says it's mine for the week and she stuffs Ben's T-shirt in a big Mulberry one. Then we leg it. I get a sort of buzz walking through the village with hundreds of quid's worth on my arm. But near home I get panicky, think I never want to go near Winnards Farm again.

Borrow it for a few days…come on…Tamara'll never know…

…but what if my mum notices? What do I say?..what do I..?

Since **when** does she notice **anything**....
..except like when you haven't done the pots..or walked the dog?

Look, your mum gets her stuff in Asda…
..Ox fam, doesn't she? She doesn't know what bloody Chloë is!

Jody…look, I'm not going there again…

You **are**! You ****ing are! You got her bag, Casey! What we take, we take back…we're borrowing…not nicking

Pretty soon Tamara's handbag starts giving me real, real creeps, like it's sort of alive. I don't want to touch it, put my hand in it. ANYTHING. I shove it under the bed in a bin bag, but even then I smell this sort of leathery breath.

Next day I'm persuading Jody we take the stuff back to the farmhouse asap. Hard work because she's like all over her handbag. Stroking it, etc. Plus she sleeps with Ben's dirty T-shirt under her pillow. Sick or what?

I just want to get rid of it, Jody!

...if you're going out, take the dog with you...

Nno...just going round Jody's, Mum....

Jody? Where're you now? Leaving the bedroom?

Okay...all clear... ...s'okay...come out now, Jody...

Did it!

Yay!

Says a lot about this boring bumhole of a village that getting in and out of someone's weekend house is exciting, but it is! We're going "omigod", our hearts are really hammering. And then on Saturday when we next see that Ben and Tamara are there we get this sneaky thrill, thinking of our little paws on their things. Pathetic, I know.

After that, every now and then (when we're sure the place is empty) Winnards Farm becomes our secret place to chill, straight after we get off the school bus. Nobody misses us. My mum's used to me doing homework round at Jody's and her mum's never home until after seven.

It's warm in the farmhouse – Tamara leaves the heating on low. We hang out in her lounge, talk about Ben (natch). Boys, pulling techniques and DOING IT (neither of us have done IT yet).

....like you don't want it to happen when you're pissed...anyway, I wouldn't do it till a boy really said he loved me...I'd wait for...

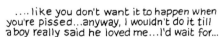

Why? Why follow boys' moves? I'm not doing that shit....I'm going to make my own moves...like do it on **my** terms...be in control...and I tell you, he'll be like **really** surprised!...he wouldn't forget it in a hurry!

Who's **HE?**

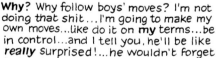

Who d'you think, you silly cow?....I want to lose my **V plates** to Ben...

Thing about Jody is, she always does what she says. She makes a plan and then does it, like when she scored in Hadditon. Not hard stuff, just blow and E. Sometimes she sniffs stuff. We never smoke at Tamara's cos of the smell. Well, as it goes, I have asthma, so shouldn't anyway.

Jody does have sane plans, like being a croupier on a liner or a computer animator. But doing it with Ben is mental! Jody says it's better doing it with him than with a boy we know. Which is true, you can't trust them, ever. Look what happened to our mate Jess. She was giving Brent a BJ and he got one of his mates to pap her on his phone, sent it ALL ROUND school.

You gotta live the DRE-E-E-AM, Case-e-e!

Imagining the first time she does it is like Jody's total obsession. I know it all backwards. She's definitely NOT doing it under the coats at a party, or in a smelly van, or a socky bedroom with his parents coming back any minute; or in a phonebox, or anywhere, anywhere near his mates.

Definitely out is doing it with someone smelling of Lynx, wearing a patterned tanga, who has loads of tatts and piercings, who does Belgian kissing (Phlegmish), who has King Kong body hair and one out of date condom. Definitely out is air punching afterwards or sniggering with his mates that he just salamied you, or guilt trips or cringey conversations like, "You won't tell anyone will you?"

This is what Jody does want: not much! Just a big empty house, a big garden, and someone well lush, buff bod (BEN!), one nice tattoo, wearing black and underneath Calvin Klein boxers, black or white. Meanwhile Jody's looking drop dead fantastic in either Tamara's black slip dress or her filmy linen shirt. There's twilight, candles, nice sheets, etc. Jody is a VISION, Ben sees her, feels her POWER. When they do it, it's like totally passionate, but also respectful. An EVENT, not just a shag. Does he text the next day? Jody says, maybe not, maybe they never meet again, it's too good to repeat.

Oh, so a one-night stand in other words...

Fuck off, Casey.

...hear Jody's hot for some older guy...so what's the goss? Is it Robbie Wray?

uh.... Dunno

You seeing her later?

uh...no... she's doing something

Sat Feb 14.

Good news. Ryan's being super-friendly. Bad news: it's not me he's after, it's Jody. That's why he's trying to find out stuff like how many Valentines she got today. Secret info: she got five – one from her mum, one from herself, one from Slimy Dean, and two mysteries – one soppy, one dirty. Either could be from Ryan, but he's not telling. And maybe he sent the anonymous text (roses r red, violets r blu, u r so fit, wanna shag u). Anyway, it'll get him nowhere.

Jody's still in fantasy land, mooning after Ben. I keep telling her, get real. It's never, ever going to happen with him. But it's no use. She loves having this BIG SECRET, thinks it dead cool having a crush on an older guy. (Not Ryan's idea of an older guy either. Robbie Wray's 19, drives a Vauxhall Nova; Ben's 27, drives a Porsche. I mean, no contest.)

'Course, I've sworn to keep shtum, so I don't tell Ryan this or let on that I'm meeting Jody at the farmhouse. She's already there, keeps texting me to hurry when all I want to do is talk to Ryan for ever! It's so-oo unfair! Why can't he be madly in lust with me and not Jody?!!? When I walk off he doesn't give me a second look.

Jody? I'll be there in three minutes...

Omigod, Jody! What the ×××× you wearing!!?

Jody's wearing all Tamara's stuff – clothes, shoes, lippy, the lot. It's like she wants to be Tamara, I mean, she's mental! Plus she's pissed. Not Tamara and Ben's booze, she says, but some she brought along, her mum's, I suppose. Or sometimes Jody gets older kids to buy it for her in the offy. Anyway, she's spilling it, and although I know Tamara and Ben are away skiing, I start getting nervous.

What she's been doing is mucking about on a laptop, that's what. The one that stays here, not the laptop Tamara takes to London. It didn't need a password, Jody got right in. Discovered loads of stuff, like Tamara's been writing a novel . . .

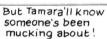

Andy: Feb 14   17.15 hrs

??!!!

I want to give you the biggest shagging of your life.

Feb 14   18.30 hrs

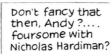

...why did Tamara do it? I just don't get it... you're a woman, Zoë...would **you** send an e-mail like that... ....to your boyfriend **AND** two other blokes?

well...if you were organising a foursome, I s'ppose...

Don't fancy that then, Andy?.... foursome with Nicholas Hardiman?

Bugger that!

Zoë.. **WHY** would she do it?...I mean, she's supposed to be marrying Ben....

well...she wants to get you all worked up...or...

...or she wants to make the boyfriend jealous ...or she's giving him a big hint she's not getting enough....or...they're kinky... or she's crazy...or she was off her face...

Reckon that's it...

She was pissed...

London E 1

Feb 14   18.30 hrs

How many times, Ben!?
I *didn't* send it! ....I can't explain it.....

...but d'you really think I'd
send you something like
that?.,..do you?

Could be somebody got at
the computer at the farm...
...but the only person with
a key is Andy...and *why*
would *he* do it??

So what am I supposed
to think?......

I dunno

..what you always think..
that I'm having loads of
affairs...that I'm going
to leave you....

I'm
not!

But you will...

What's that's supposed to mean!?....
Just because Fran left you...

Leave Fran
out of it!

No I won't! That's
what this is about,
isn't it?

Fran's always at the back of your
mind, isn't she?...I *know* she is! It's
like another person in the room...

You're not over her, are you?...I'm
bloody sick of it!.....if you had
Something to do, you wouldn't
Spend so much time moping about!

Where're you
going?

Out

Beth: Feb 16

I deleted Tamara's message to Nicholas at **ONCE!**

I thought, "Tamara, you stupid, stupid little tart, what ARE you playing at?"
I know some people will think I've no right, no right at all to censor my husband's e-mails, but I can't risk his being distracted. I want him to finish the novel.
I just want it over, done. I want Nicholas back.
In the ordinary way I love authors in the throes of writing.
Well, I should do, since that's our aim at Stonefield, to provide a perfect creative atmosphere.
A writer totally immersed in their own little universe pleases me no end.
It means I've succeeded.
 Outside, stuff happens.
 Inside nothing much shakes their world, and, if it does, in two minutes everything settles.

With this book of Nick's, things feel different.
His detachment seems greater and . . .
I may as well be frank: often at
a certain stage of a book our sex life
goes on hold, but this time it . . .
No, actually I don't want to talk
about it. All I will say is that
when I put Nick's words on
the computer, and his main

characters are going at it like express trains, it's pretty hard to take.
And as for Tamara Drewe inviting him and Andy to some crazy shagfest – *how crass is that?*

Are the cows looking well? Wouldn't know, Andy...I hardly notice them...are they always the same ones?....or are they refills?

Before you go, Nicholas ...uh...what did you make of Tamara's e-mail?

Uh?

Tamara...she sent us...you and me, an e-mail, right?

Really?

Oh, Beth deals with all that...it'll be in her pile of print-outs...

Don't think she'd care to print this one out, Nicholas...

by Tamara Drewe

This week life has become a bit like the plot of a Mozart opera. You know the kind, where letters written as if from The Beloved fall into the wrong hands and cause maximum mayhem. In my case it wasn't a letter but a rogue e-mail. It was sent on my computer (not by me – honest) to the Man in my Life and to two other men in my address book (one I hardly know) telling them in so many words that I want to give them a bit of legover.

O.K. It was Valentine's Day, so the Boyfriend did have reason to expect something. But he simply wouldn't believe me. If it had been a handwritten letter he would have seen at once that it was a forgery. In the case of an electronic message, it's strange how we never doubt the authenticity of its source. In spite of all my denials the Boyfriend got the hump. He's gone off, two days so far.

Nobody told me that the reason men are so suspicious is just that they are made like that, nothing we can do, ried, after years of staying res-

...yeah, well...you'll just have to believe me, Andy...it's just a mystery.... I **never** sent it

..but only if you have time...

...just take a look in the house...see if anyone's been in...

rRr-ring!!

Who is it?

Me

Ben! Omigod!

Casey:

After Jody sent her stupid e-mail, we kept away from Winnards Farm. I don't know what we expected to happen – the police testing Tamara's laptop for fingerprints, sussing us, coming round and doing us for breaking in. Well, that didn't happen, but we should be careful. I mean, we're back using the old bus shelter, where you get a good view up the lane. Today we saw the old writer guy from Stonefield go past Winnards Farm – very slowly, like he was really really interested.

..But d'you wax off **ALL** of it?

No...you leave a little strip in the front, says here...

God, it'd be like velcro...

Eww...check the cellulite on her!...been sitting on a bead car-seat cover or **what**?!

I tell Jody we should hang out somewhere else, and she goes, "Like where, your bloody bedroom?" Which is true. It's so-ooo boring, this village. Nowhere to go, nothing to do. Nothing happening, except when Gary Pound and his mates nearly set fire to the Coronation Tree on the green.

So, I'm thinking OK, might as well go home, do some homework, because Jody's getting up my nose, too. She's droning on about Ben, Ben all the time. But if I even mention Ryan or boys at school she starts dissing them, treating me like a moron.

You don't know what you'd be letting yourself in for, Casey....
...they can't kiss...

Snog Ryan...bet you ...he'd be like a donkey eating an apple....

You just have no idea, Casey, do you? Kissing's an art...

Oh yeah? How would you know? You're not getting any...

...What you reckon, Casey?....
her extensions synthetic or what? Couldn't be real...too long!

Omigod! Jody!

It's **him!** Look!! It's Ben!

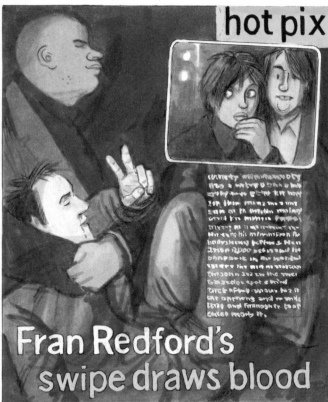

hot pix

Fran Redford's swipe draws blood

SKYE BOLTON'S BABY BUMP?!

KARI LAUGHS OFF SPLIT RUMOURS

OI! GET A ROOM!
PRESTON KAY & MOFFAT LEE'S PUBLIC TONGUE-FEST

32 A TO 38 EE
KERRON CHECKS OUT ROXI'S BRAND NEW BAPS

goss 33

"Ex Swipe drummer, Ben Sergeant nurses a bloody nose outside London's Komodo bar...after a pavement spat with songstress and former long-term love, Fran Redford...

"...ended in blows, when doorstaff intervened... Friends say the row erupted because Ben's still sore at Fran's dumping him for fellow Swipe, Steve Culley....and while Fran's career is on a high, Ben's took a dive when he left the band....."

"Fran will always care for Ben", said a source, " but right now, she's giving 100% to her relationship with Steve."

I knew it! I knew he would be! God, Casey, Ben's really, really **romantic**... like he really **loved** Fran! He's romantic ...he's not just a serial shagger!

So...what you reckon, Jody? Tamara'll dump him now, yeah? Then he won't come here any more...

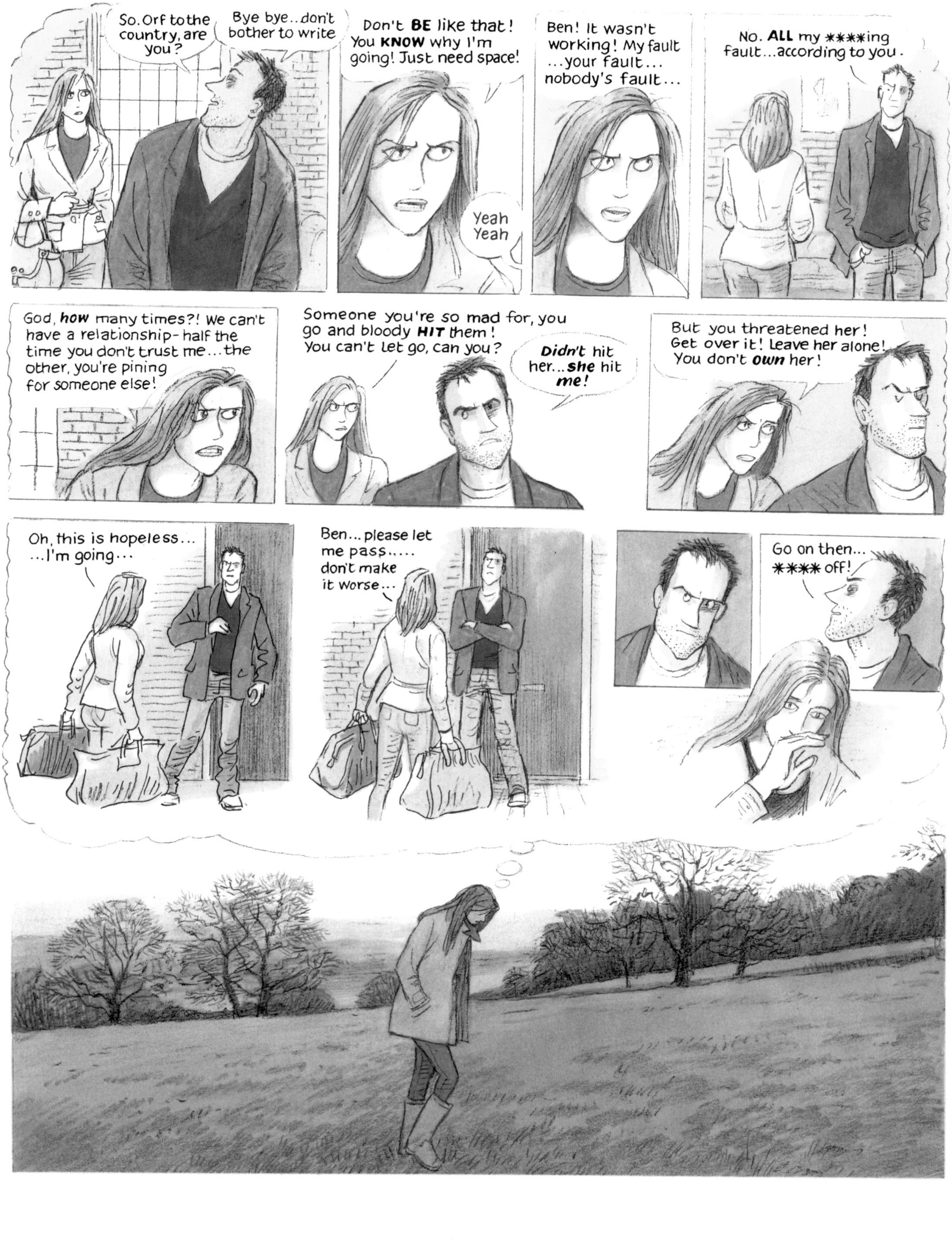

So. Orf to the country, are you?
Bye bye.. don't bother to write
Don't **BE** like that! You **KNOW** why I'm going! Just need space!
Yeah Yeah
Ben! It wasn't working! My fault ...your fault... nobody's fault...
No. **ALL** my ✱✱✱✱ing fault...according to you.
God, **how** many times?! We can't have a relationship - half the time you don't trust me...the other, you're pining for someone else!
Someone you're so mad for, you go and bloody **HIT** them! You can't let go, can you?
Didn't hit her...***she*** hit ***me!***
But you threatened her! Get over it! Leave her alone! You don't ***own*** her!
Oh, this is hopeless... ...I'm going...
Ben... please let me pass..... don't make it worse...
Go on then... ✱✱✱✱ off!

I'm transcribing the handwriters' output for the day – 3½ pages from Nicholas and a couple of long chapters from Ingrid, who's here for a week. Nicholas keeps complaining we attract too many writers like her. He refers to them as UFFs – Unpublished, Fiftyish Females – usually very keen on Creativity Exercises and keeping Dream Diaries. (They can also be male, but we don't see many at Stonefield.)

 Nicholas likes me to edit his work as I go along. Here everything's fine except for the last half page. There's a sudden stream of consciousness in a voice I don't recognise at all. Perhaps it's a new character to go in later, or Nick forgot to leave me everything.

> She gets a tick in all the boxes — loyal, he[l]...
> *sp* amiable, reliable, helpful, discreet
> etc — and she irritates me to Hell!
>
> *?* I Don't show it because I can't take the fall-out yet. I have to wait till the book's done. And she tolerates it — my silences, evasions, ingratitude — so I feel guilty and even more irritated.
> Don't want to spoil things for her — she enjoys our life. Finds it rich and full — likes the familiar, the predictable —— while I ——
> I find it empty. Dull. Dead.
> Every morning I wake with the same thought, like a mantra — Is this ALL? Is this ALL?

?? where does this go?

It's me...

It's only on second reading I realise that I've scooped up from Nick's desk something which can't be fiction, which isn't meant for my eyes and which after a minute I tear into tiny pieces and put on the fire in the Reading Room.

 Then Ingrid comes in wanting to borrow binoculars and to know if the birds in Home Field were rooks or crows, and were they a bad omen? I say, probably a bad omen, if you believe that sort of thing.

Are they rooks?

Let's have a look...

It's just that I want to get the details absolutely right for the country scene I'm doing....

Well, I'm sure they're rooks

Hm..little speck of red out there...

Mn... ..oh

Just my husband out for a walk.

Even though we agree to take turns, Jody usually waits for me to call – so my moby costs a bomb! And she never ever rings the weekends I'm at my Dad and stepmum's, maybe 'cos she's super-sensitive about not wanting to see her dad much. Well, he is miles away. Also his girl friend had twin girls last year and all the ickle baba-goo-goo does Jody's head in.

Anyway, this weekend I'm at my dad's and Jody's like non stop texting and phoning. About Tamara and Ben, natch. Well, zero Ben sightings! So looks like their relationship's really gone into melt-down and they've split. Tamara's been on her own at the farm, hasn't moved her car. (Jody put little balls of mud in front of the tyres and they're still there.) And Jody saw her up in the window checking herself in the mirror for AGES, looking really, really gutted.

Jody doesn't agree, but I think Ben's a total Love Rat. I reckon Tamara should move on, because he's just not into her any more. She should get over it, maybe have a fantastic makeover, like Cherelle had after Sol Kidd dumped her. Maybe go blonde and have her tits done or Botox whatever. Except Tamara's tits look OK, in fact she's 95% well fit, got everything. Except a boyfriend of course.

But if Tamara's been throwing little pity-parties for herself, it's nothing to what Jody does. She's such a drama-queen. I mean, you'd think it was HER that Ben dumped, not Tamara.

Our next Tamara sighting's Tuesday, after school. We're having a smoke on The Log and suddenly she comes in the field, her hair all skanky and looking really pissed off. Well, like you would do if you've been Betrayed.

They talked for about three minutes, then Tamara turns round and comes past us back to the farm. Maybe she only needed a short walk or maybe she didn't fancy going into the long field where the cows are. I don't. But did she meet the bloke by chance or did she plan it? Maybe Jody's e-mail set off something. Maybe he rattles her cage!

Beth...it's me...yes... I've only **just** left the London Library...

...so I may be later than I said...yes, the rush hour, too....no, don't wait for me...I'll have it when I get in...OK?

Two days later

Exactly a year ago I subscribed to the caucasian ideal: I underwent rhinoplasty, in other words, a nose job. I traded up, had my bulbous conk sculpted into a smaller, neater model for entirely respectable reasons: higher self-esteem, the wish to look NORMAL. But I tell a lie. No way did I want to look normal, average! Exceptional more like. Exceptionally attractive, if at all possible. Well, I'm not boasting, but my surgeon did a really fantastic job. These days I turn heads.

And is life better as one of the more-than-averagely attractive? Yes and no. You get ogled more, you get more sexual

AWAY FROM IT ALL

by Tamara Drewe

offers. But not necessarily better sex, perhaps because men have higher expectations of beautiful women. As for Love, well everyone knows Beauty's no

guarantor of durable relationships. As I mentioned last week, my boyfriend's dumped me.

I'm not saying that I hanker for my old nose, but I realise how much I blamed it in the past for romantic setbacks. (If it wasn't for my nose he'd love me.) That's the lure of surgery. For the plain and ugly it offers improvement, the chance of a new, more loveable you. But for the Beautiful, surgery is a sign of deterioration, a clumsy attempt to maintain the Perfect. A losing battle. That's why we should all learn to admire Inner Beauty, the kind that really matters. Or so I'm told.

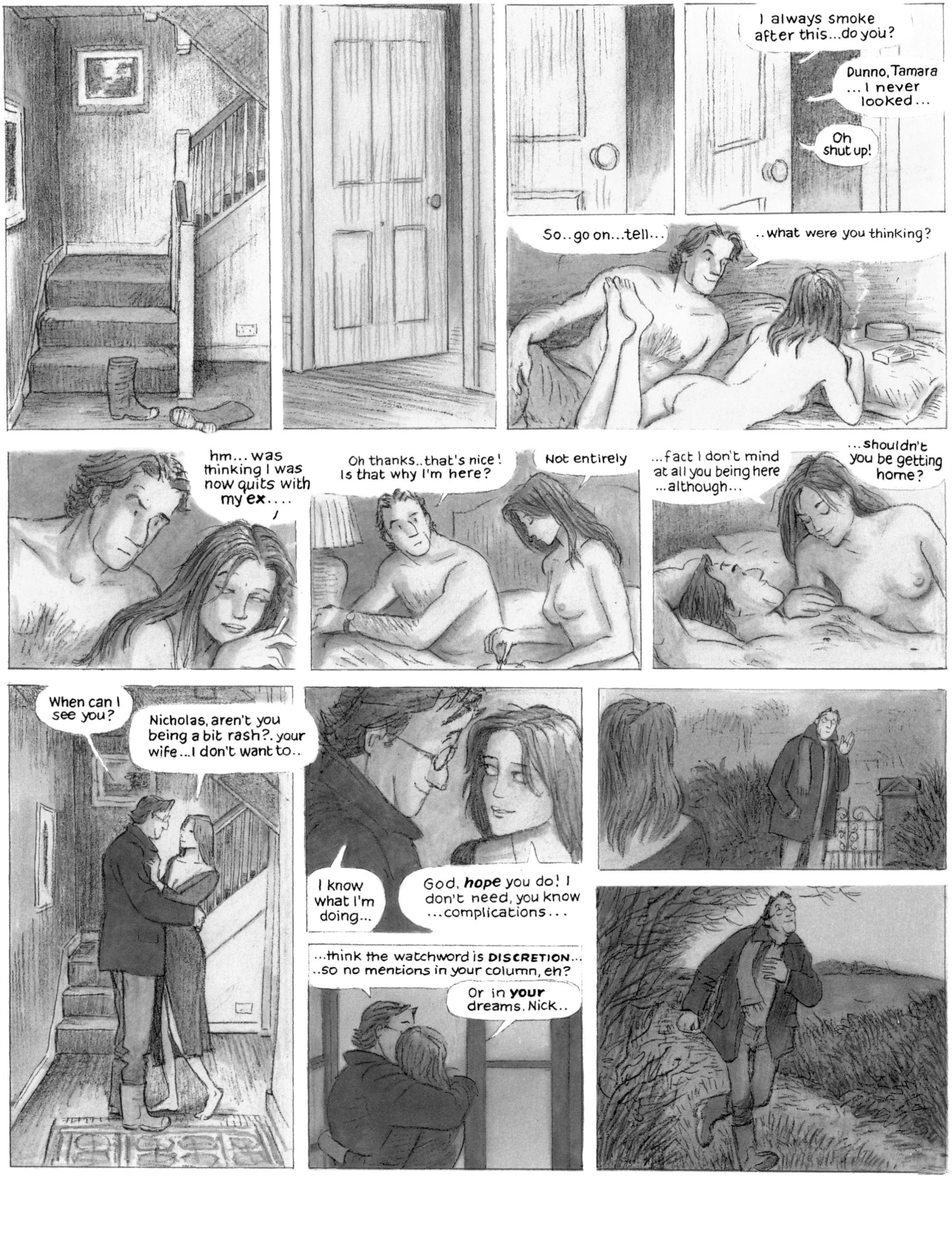
I always smoke after this...do you?
Dunno, Tamara ... I never looked...
Oh shut up!
So..go on...tell...
..what were you thinking?
hm... was thinking I was now quits with my ex....
Oh thanks..that's nice! Is that why I'm here?
Not entirely
...fact I don't mind at all you being here ...although...
...shouldn't you be getting home?
When can I see you?
Nicholas, aren't you being a bit rash?. your wife...I don't want to..
I know what I'm doing...
God, hope you do! I don't need, you know ...complications...
...think the watchword is DISCRETION... ..so no mentions in your column, eh?
Or in your dreams, Nick..

Hii!

Nick! O good

Was it awful?

Oh...coming out of London was...but after that, very little traffic

Oh it's nothing...I just nipped into Fortnum's on my way to the Library...

mmh!...all my favourite teas!

FORTNUM & MASON
Green Teas
GUNPOWDER

It's wonderful, Nick in a good mood. The difference between Nick this morning and Nick now is extraordinary. He's like my electric toothbrush after I've recharged it.

I tell him he ought to have a day in London more often and he agrees. It gives him a buzz.

He asks, "Any messages?"

Well, there is something irritating (from his point of view): the Monksted Literary Festival has sent details of Nick's event there next month. Not only do they want him to share a platform with another writer, but they've booked him into some crummy pub, not Boldwood Manor, as usual. I expect fireworks, but Nick's very cheery about it, says he'll sort it out.

And so we join the writers in the kitchen, where they've got as far as the cheese. Nicholas plonks himself next to Lillian (who I know he thinks a frightful pain in the arse) and goes on to amuse and charm her pants off – and everyone else's.

Wonderful Paella, Beth!

...Gosh, would you *really*? Ooh, that would be *soo-oo* kind...to have an expert eye! ...I must explain that *AFTER* chapter two...there's a bit of...uh...*magic realism*...and that's sort of the key to

SPRING

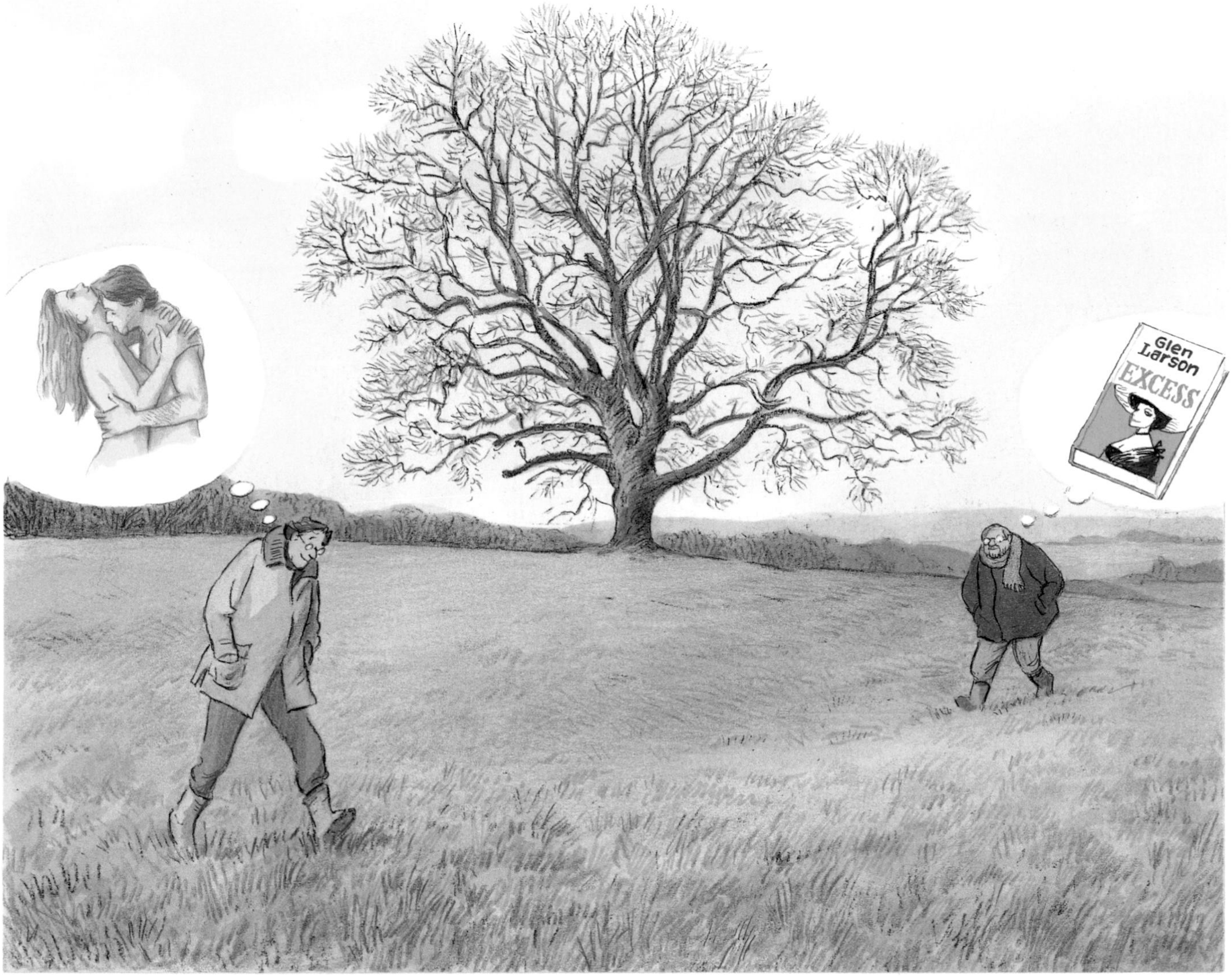
Glen Larson
EXCESS

In the months away from Stonefield I hardly wrote a chapter. Paris was great for research but just too full of agreeable distraction. As for London, well, Maggie and I have got it together again and, while this is nice from every warm, fond, companionly aspect, it hasn't been ideal for the book. It's not that Maggie ever says anything, but when I close the door of the room where I work, I have the feeling that I'm shutting her out. (Unlike Beth. There's a woman who doesn't mind how long you cloister yourself.)

As planned, here I am again at Stonefield, far from the madding crowd, back in my cozy barn, my womb within a womb. And within two days my novel has roared into life, so much so that I promised my editor at Fantail – and yes, after years of radio silence, we're now in the most eager contact – I promised her that eight weeks more of solid grind would do it. I shall deliver in May, publish in the Fall.

Life has rarely felt so good. Fruitful hours at my desk, a gentle stroll, a doze in the Reading Room, a trip to the store, and very often a chat in Beth's peaceful kitchen. Sometimes no chat at all. Just our own pleasant thoughts.

Beth:

I suspect Nicholas is having another affair. Not the kind he lets me know about, the other kind. I have no evidence, not a scrap, just that feeling in my bones, the feeling I seem incapable of ignoring. I despise myself. If I let it, this tiny twinge will soon become the full-blown thing, the sordid thing of suspecting, watching, checking. Before I know it, I'll be going through his pockets. It's disgusting, mortifying. Madness.

I tell myself to get a grip. I can't pin anything on Nick. But that's what can be suspicious. Look, I'm married to someone who spends his life inventing ways of concealing and detecting foul play. There's no one to beat Nick's villains for covering their tracks, no one either to beat Dr Inchcombe for smelling a rat.

And that's what I must do, stop sniffing for rats. Nicholas is pretty well in purdah trying to finish his book. He does nothing else, not even his chores. Glen has taken to doing them: gets the wine out, fills the log basket, carries the shopping. He says it's soothing after a day at the laptop. And I find Glen soothing.

The other day we spotted Tamara in Tesco. She didn't see us, and I told Glen about the stupid e-mails she sent to Nick and Andy, and how I don't feel that friendly, even though I suppose it was a joke. A joke that backfired. She's been on about it in her column: it seems her boyfriend dumped her.

Oh, so she's on the loose... She after Andy now?

No, I don't think so... He doesn't work for her any more... he didn't know she'd split with Ben, till I told him....

Yes...he's history, apparently

!

Jody and me, we were going to watch this slushy vid last night. But Jody didn't show, didn't phone, no text, nothing. And today she wasn't in school, so like I was really worried. Then at lunch break she texts. She's really, really ill – mega food poisoning, she wants to die and stuff. Bit later she texts about us meeting here. Now she's just fessed up. Total bollocks about food poisoning. She was round at Katy Pound's necking vodka – 2 bottles, she says. So I go, you cow, you total scuzzbag.

Andy kicks the Land-Rover before he leaves and we're like, "What did she say to him?" And a few minutes later we see Tamara's door opening again . . .

Tamara having it off with Nick Hardiman is like, wow, hot news, but totally gross as well. He's so-oo old! Jody is really upset, it really bugs her. And I know why: because of her dad going off with someone loads younger. I remember the weekend when she heard his girlfriend was up the duff. Jody was mental, got really bladdered, had to be put to bed with a bucket.

We google "nicholas hardiman". He's 55, so younger than Michael Douglas, for instance. And he's much more famous than we thought, written loads of books which've been on telly. My mum and Nan watched "Doctor Inchcombe". So he is a sort of celeb, maybe D-list. Even so, Jody thinks it's well sick, thinks Tamara a bit of a slag. But I don't. I mean, what is a slag? You'd think it meant going with lots of guys or doing it for money or doing it with someone you just met. Actually it's more complicated. Like, Katy Pound's sister is a slag for doing it once with Jeff Price after he lied he loved her. But Tivoli Garnier ISN'T, when she's like full-on with a different guy every week. Weird.

GOSS / 45

File WHO's doing WHO?

The other crap thing about Tamara and Nick Hardiman is him being married. So he's a right cheating bastard, like Jody's dad. Well, and mine too, except Mum says she was bored with him ages before he met my step-mum.

I know Nick's wife's called Beth. She's coming up the road, probably to the post-box. You don't see posh people on foot in Ewedown. Mostly they tool about in massive 4 by 4s. But we often see her. Usually she says "Hi", or something. She's one of the few people who don't look at us like we need locking up.

It's weird knowing something that maybe she doesn't. I'm really into stories. My mum says I always ruin soaps on telly cos I suss what's going to happen, like I know what's going to hit Beth soon. Tamara and Nick get too Loved-Up to hide it – like Brad and

It's like I can't look till she's gone past. I feel sort of horrible – dunno, sort of upset for her.

Angelina. Then it All Comes Out, then the Divorce, then Beth's world falls apart till she moves on, puts the bitterness behind her. Usually the story's better with someone young cos they get to fall in love with someone else, etc.

Thing is, now, I don't know if Beth says "Hi" to us or not.

Nicholas has at last finished work on his book and my God, he's being nice. Really kind and thoughtful. Thing is, I still don't know if it's out of gratitude for my loving support, or adulterous guilt. I just can't tell. That's why I'm re-reading one of his earlier books, the one with the cheating husband, Theo, who "loved adultery not just for the physical thrill, but much more for the battle of wits, the secrecy, the grubby hole-in-the-cornerness of it all".

Thanks to the list of Golden Rules, (eg, "to allay suspicion, first arouse it", then "prove your alibi") and his genius for games of deception ("Lulling the Spouse"), Theo's wife remains unaware of his peccadilloes, until the end when she runs him through with a carving knife. Now, I believe Nicholas and I played at "Lulling the Spouse" on Tuesday.

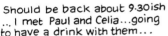

Nicholas has been doing this a lot recently. Telling the truth, lulling me.
After a bit you stop checking – It's too humiliating. He's always where he says he will be, all innocent and plausible.

Hang on, Cate...we'll go home that way...not going in there...those cows are really scary...

OK, so go on, Tamara...you say it's not serious?

No...don't want anything serious for a bit...you know, after Ben..... Just want some good, clean fun that's all...

Still...quite a notch on your bed post... Nicholas Hardiman

Yeah...it *is* sort of flattering... Thing is, I'm learning stuff...he's so disciplined! He writes *every* day for **5** hours!.....I want him to read my novel, so far....

So, what about his wife?

Oh, I'm not spoiling anything there ...they've been married yonks...she does her thing, he does his. They're more like friends...

Except Nick is really *paranoid* about her finding out...so, keep your mouth shut, Cate!

Oh my lips are sealed

S'funny, right from word go, he said **NO** texts, **no** e-mails, phone calls...**no** letters....

Pity...I'd like letters from him

So, **how** d'you arrange things?

There's a lamp in the window...

He passes here same time, twice a week ...if the lamp's on, he knows he can come in... if it's off, he knows there's a problem...

See this bit of chalk?

Yeh?

...If there's a problem...I'll suggest other times for him to tick....

God, Tamara, you're barking! What a palaver! What happens when you have a row?...One of you gets bored...or forgets? Or goes under a bus?

Dunno...cross that bridge when I come to it...all good things come to an end...

My birthday is two days after Jody's and we both get upgrades on our mobys. Mine's not as cool as the one Jody's dad gives her, but it's really OK, with a camera, zoom and stuff.

So we've been hanging out being like paparazzi, taking hot paps of people – well, hot in our dreams. The waiting gets really really boring and all we pap is things like Nick Hardiman's wife posting letters or someone in our class showing off her hickies.

On Saturday we get a lift into Hadditon but can't get one back and have to get the bus, a real bummer – buses don't go to Ewedown any more, means walking bloody miles from the crossroads.

On top of that, Nipper, Terry, etc. are on the bus and they're like infants, total dipsticks, think they're so-o cool cos they got spraypaint and a load of 18-rated games in the market.

Jody's

casey's

Shireway

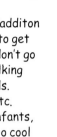
...oi scene queens! fat arse!..talkin' to you...

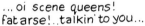
✳✳✳✳ off and die!

?
!

Omigod, Jody! It's **his!** ...Nick Hardiman's, innit?

What you reckon? s'abandoned... yeah?

It's **parked!** Not ✳✳✳✳ing abandoned, you dork!....**What** you **doing??!**

Nipper etc. do their number, let all the tyres down and leg it. They are so-o tragic. I want to leg it too, but Jody wants to hang around. She says, "It could be well interesting, could be a great papping opportunity." Winnards Farm is just up the road – which is where Nick Hardiman must be, getting all down and dirty with Tamara.
So we hide in the bushes and wait, and wait.

How long're we gonna wait?... :Tsk: taking his time

He's a perve. ...I hate him

You **hate** him? Why?

Cos he's a cheater... like my dad

Ssh!

＊⦿＊!!＊

Tamara... yeah, I know...I'm phoning and I shouldn't, but this is an emergency.∴ You haven't got a foot pump, have you?...Some sod's let down all my...You **have**!? You're a wonder! Yes...I'm just up the road on the right....

Beth, hi...I said I'd be back at 4... ...be more like **5**...yes, I'm still on the motorway....**what**? You can hear **what**? **ROOKS**? Really? You're hearing things.... ...See you soon....

We have to crouch down really low because Nick starts peering about. Then we hear Tamara arrive, then him pumping up the tyres, which goes on for about 10 years. Next peek, both of them're looking at the bushes, all nervous. And we're like having a nervy b., cos all twigs and stuff start cracking every time we move. Jody gets pins and needles and dead legs.
So it's ME that paps them, me – when they're certainly not looking. And it's this totally mega, mega pap!

Go! Casey!! Do it! Do it!

Take care

Come on Casey... it's OK!

We're inside Winnards Farm. I just knew Jody wouldn't be able to keep out of here. All week she's been going, "What they doing? "What's happening?" like Tamara and Nick live in Soapland.

Today we saw Tamara's car wasn't there, the windows all shut and the spare key still under the pot out the back. I was bottling about the alarm, but as usual it wasn't set. Tamara never bothers, I suppose no point, cos the police take 50 million years to get here from Hadditon. So here I am being lookout while Jody goes from room to room touching stuff, like it's lucky.

Imagine being her! Imagine having all this, Casey... Imagine doing it here

..Imagine doing it..... with Ben...imagine the first time...

I don't want to imagine anything in the bedroom, what with Nick Hardiman using it now, and stuff. Why is Jody still obsessing? If it ever happened, and it won't, why would doing it with Ben, HERE, be so great? What difference would a load of poncey cushions make? You can have a cringey time anywhere. And it would be cringey, Jody should know, she's never done IT. Furthest she's ever gone was with Sam. Clothes on, zip stuff. Patted the dog through the letterbox. That was before she found out Sam was two-timing her with Lisa, who's a real minger.

I want to go. I HATE being here.

Ever tried this, Casey?..Calvados? S'like brandy...

Ooh, tried this? computer cleaner ...gives you a good...

How 'bout it, Case? Have a little puff.....

Oh God!

Jody! I want to GO!! Anyway, you know I can't with my asth...

Asthma! Tsk, you're just a ✳✳✳✳ing wuss!.....

No, no Casey!...Casee!... I'm kidding...I didn't mean it! Really!...Sorry...come on, have a drink, then....

NO!

Look, I want to GO!!

OK! OK! When I've checked something.... OK?

Tamara's stuff is all over the kitchen table. We check her diary to see if it's windowed-out with Nick dates, but there's nothing except a weekend in April: "Nick/Lit Fest," it says, plus how to get to Boldwood Manor Hotel. On Tamara's laptop there's nothing to or from Nick either. Really weird, since they're so loved-up. But there are two e-mails from Ben, a couple of weeks apart, and these get Jody really, really going.

Tamara
You say there is no one else, but you can't see me - do you mean can't or don't want to see me?
Try being honest. Ben

Big big favour to ask. Would you be willing to look after the dog while I'm in L.A. 3 months max, Apr - July. My dad can't have him. Don't want to put Boss in kennels. Know he liked you, you him. Ben

Dear Ben
OK I don't want to see you. I need space and I don't need any more e-mails about what went wrong between us. I don't mean I don't ever want to see you, just not for a while.
Tamara

Ben. re Boss. Very sorry, I can't. I don't know what my plans are this summer.
T

Dear Ben
Have found really reliable dog-lover in the village who would love to look after Boss. Please deal directly with Jody on 07642 998096.
Tamara

There...sent... now delete...

But what'll your mum say?! Bloody great dog! God, Jody, you're really serious about seeing Ben, aren't you?!

I go to the post a lot these days. Anything to get out of Stonefield. I'm fed up, fed up with Nicholas. The other day I caught him looking at me the way I look at him when his back is turned. I said pointedly, "D'you want to tell me something?" He snapped, "Beth, don't start all that again."

So I let it go, thought OK, fine, at least Suspicion's out in the open now: he'll find it harder to tell lies. But now I think, what am I doing playing games? I'm fed up. The writers depress me, their self-importance, their martyrishness – no one asks them to write 800 pages. And I'm fed up with the silence here. Not that the village is any more lively, especially Monday to Friday when the weekenders aren't there. The only faces I see are the local kids, sometimes the two girls, sometimes others, hanging around bored witless, waiting for something to happen, I suppose. I have to steel myself because they hardly ever say "Hallo" back. But I notice there's always a stir and nudges when I pass. God, life must be dull if they find ME interesting.

Come on, Casey.. **DO** it! He's a pig!...
... **I'll** do it, if you won't...

I've just seen Nicholas off to London, where he's staying in the flat for a couple of days. Our daughter Lulu lives there too, so he can't get up to much. But then he goes on to Monksted and that's a different matter. The first literary festival of the year. Nicholas has a room at Boldwood Manor, I know because I booked it. He has two events, one on Sunday and a panel discussion on the Monday, plus invitations to three select parties.

Sounds nice, doesn't it? The reality is horrible. I HATE festivals . . . rutting grounds of viciousness, jealousy, vanity, disgusting displays of male ego – well, and female – "My queue's longer than your queue", etc. Loathsome.
Anyway, I punish Nicholas – for whatever I'm sure he'll get up to – with a guilt-provoking show of sweetness and efficiency.

Here we are . . . all in here . . . timings, itinerary, contact numbers . . . ..so have a lovely, lovely time . . .

You **ARE** an angel!

You're a marvel!

I fume in the kitchen. I know I asked for it, but he called me "a marvel" – the same way he thanked our cleaner when she found his missing chequebook. *That's the sort of pat on the head you get if you do nurturing, doormat sort of work. Useful of course, we're very, very useful . . . No good blaming feminists for giving "women's work" a bad image. . . . When have men ever valued it?*

My thoughts are interrupted by a chirrup from my mobile, and Andy coming in for his money.

! ! !

Omigod!!

OhH! **HER!** God! Her . . . and him!! Bastard!! OhH . . . OhH..

Tsk! Ohh! . . help me Andy . . . who sent this ? . . how do I find out . . . . ?

. . . says caller withheld . . . so dunno . . .

...got nice spinach... pick you some, drop it round later?

No thanks, Andy... just the eggs... See you...

Tamara...

What?

..uh..I wanted a word

Oh?

You and Nicholas...

What're you talking about?

Come on...you know what I mean....and I don't think much of it....

Couldn't care less what you think... *None* of your bloody business, Andy!

OK... forget it.

Wait! Andy! *What* d'you know? *WHO* told you?

No one **TOLD** me...I put two and two together.

Andy, it's **NOTHING TO DO WITH YOU!**.... ..You've no right to...

Oh I think I do!...I care a lot for Beth....her marriage being screwed up...

Oh for Godsake! It's **not** like that! I've no intention of breaking them up... It's nothing serious.... It's just...

Bit of fun, eh?

What you playing at, Tamara? Why **HIM**? Why **Nicholas**?...when you could have **ANYONE**? - You only got to bat your eyes....

What's in it for you, eh?

Well, I know Nicholas...he done this before... He's a right bugger...likes having his cake and eating it....

And you like being that, do you? His bit of secret nooky.... Doesn't have to go far, does he? Nice and handy...

Shuddup Andy!

Why you saying this!? You're just jealous of him, aren't you!? **Aren't you!?**

Just *piss* off!

Oh, I will!

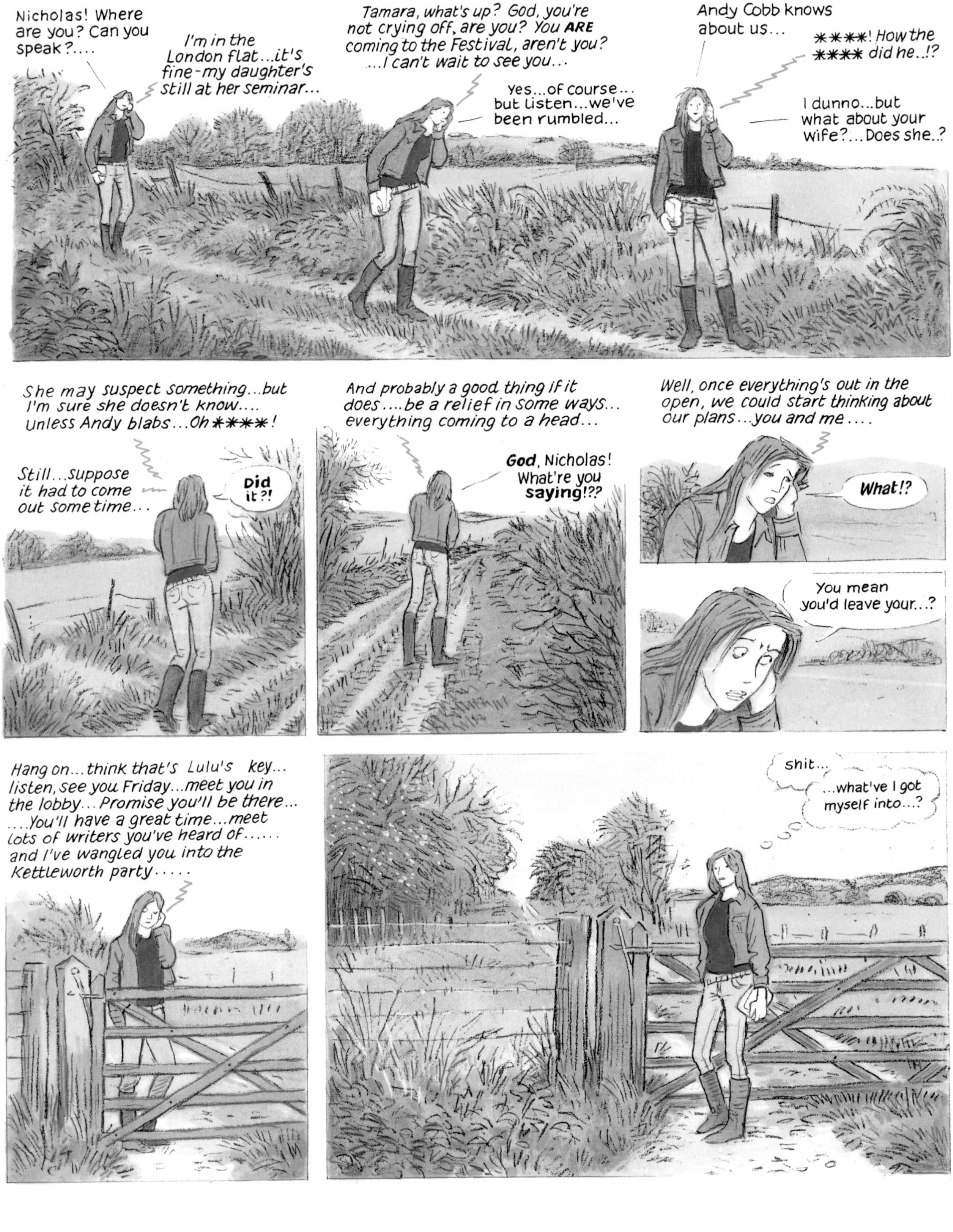
Nicholas! Where are you? Can you speak?....
I'm in the London flat...it's fine-my daughter's still at her seminar...
Tamara, what's up? God, you're not crying off, are you? You ARE coming to the Festival, aren't you? ...I can't wait to see you...
Yes...of course... but listen...we've been rumbled...
Andy Cobb knows about us...
****! How the **** did he..!?
I dunno...but what about your wife?...Does she..?
She may suspect something...but I'm sure she doesn't know.... Unless Andy blabs...Oh ****!
Still...suppose it had to come out some time...
Did it?!
And probably a good thing if it does....be a relief in some ways... everything coming to a head...
God, Nicholas! What're you saying!??
Well, once everything's out in the open, we could start thinking about our plans...you and me....
What!?
You mean you'd leave your...?
Hang on...think that's Lulu's key... listen, see you Friday...meet you in the lobby... Promise you'll be there... ...You'll have a great time...meet lots of writers you've heard of...... and I've wangled you into the Kettleworth party.....
shit...
...what've I got myself into...?

Excuse me, girls...but did one of you send me something on my phone the other day?

we wot?

Nno.. sorry.

You quite sure?..... OK...never mind... sorry to bother you.

S'OK

Those girls are lying. I'm sure they know when and where Nicholas saw that bitch. Which is more than I do, even though I've rooted shamelessly through his things. He rings every night – yesterday to say that he'd be home in time for the crime writers next Saturday. When we speak I never give him the slightest hint that I know about him and Tamara. I'm not going to humiliate myself by forcing it out of him. No, I want *him* to have to to tell me. So I hold my fire, bide my time, don't set fire to Tamara's house or scream obscenities at her or do anything rash.

Except on Tuesday, seeing her car in Hadditon, I couldn't help it. I nipped into the deli and got some fish stock cubes and crumbled them down the air intake. A damp, chilly day. With the heater on – a good stink. And today, replying to Nicholas's fan mail, I couldn't help myself either. I am so angry.

...the way they always look at me...

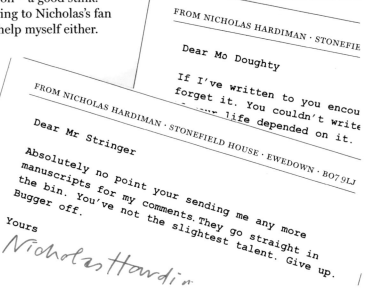

FROM NICHOLAS HARDIMAN · STONEFIE

Dear Mo Doughty

If I've written to you encou
forget it. You couldn't write
your life depended on it.

FROM NICHOLAS HARDIMAN · STONEFIELD HOUSE · EWEDOWN · BO7 9LJ

Dear Mr Stringer

Absolutely no point your sending me any more
manuscripts for my comments. They go straight in
the bin. You've not the slightest talent. Give up.
Bugger off.

Yours

Nicholas Hardin

Monksted used to be Nicholas's favourite festival: small, select, everyone a proper writer. No telly chefs, comics, gardeners or tit-queens. (True, some of the more august literati could sniff at Nick, find him tainted with populism, but he used to console himself – his sales were ten times bigger than theirs.)
Anyway, times change.

Sunday   MAIN MARQUEE (£8.00)
6pm   **Jean-Patrice Le Coq**
            The celebrated chef, sex-symbol and presenter of *à Table* in conversation with Fenella Cloud

6pm   COSSINGTON MARQUEE (£6.00)
            Nicholas Hardiman
            The creator of Dr Inchcombe talks with Lucia Dodd about the craft of crime writing and the experience of being adapted for TV

All weekend not a minute goes by when I'm not thinking of Nicholas's schedule: of the party in the Long Room, 19.00 to 21.30 on Saturday; the BBC 4 interview, in the Library, Sunday 11.30; local radio interview, 14.30; pre-event rendezvous, Green Room tent, 17.30.

...it always happens... on at the same time as some ****ing chef!

Oh you'll be OK, Nick...

I'm indistinguishable from 95 per cent of the women at the festival, but almost immediately Tamara Drewe's gaze locks on to mine.

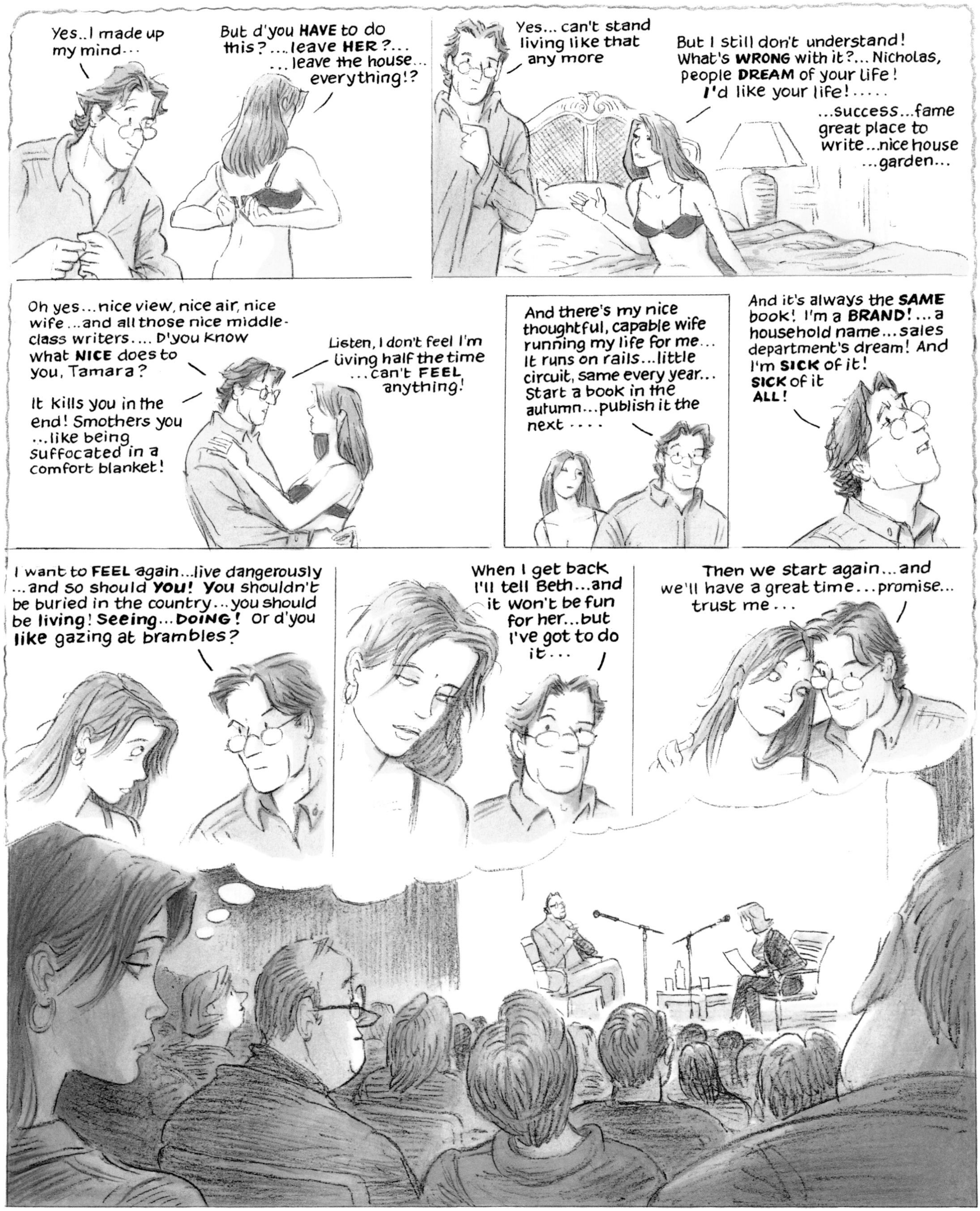

Yes..I made up my mind...
But d'you HAVE to do this?....leave HER?... ...leave the house... everything!?
Yes... can't stand living like that any more
But I still don't understand! What's WRONG with it?... Nicholas, people DREAM of your life! I'd like your life!.....
...success...fame great place to write...nice house ...garden...
Oh yes...nice view, nice air, nice wife...and all those nice middle-class writers.... D'you know what NICE does to you, Tamara?
It kills you in the end! Smothers you ...like being suffocated in a comfort blanket!
Listen, I don't feel I'm living half the time ...can't FEEL anything!
And there's my nice thoughtful, capable wife running my life for me... It runs on rails...little circuit, same every year... Start a book in the autumn...publish it the next....
And it's always the SAME book! I'm a BRAND!...a household name...sales department's dream! And I'm SICK of it! SICK of it ALL!
I want to FEEL again...live dangerously ...and so should YOU! You shouldn't be buried in the country...you should be living! Seeing...DOING! Or d'you like gazing at brambles?
When I get back I'll tell Beth...and it won't be fun for her...but I've got to do it...
Then we start again...and we'll have a great time...promise... trust me...

I can't see where Tamara's sitting – somewhere behind me. She stays for Nicholas's talk, but not for the questions. I see her slip out of the tent during the applause – and there's a lot of that. Audiences tend to love Nicholas and usually I'm proud of him. But today, watching him soak in that warm bath of approval I could fill a sick bag, smug, lying, two-faced . . .

...OK...another question...
...Lady at the side there...

You write a lot about adultery... Is it from personal experience?

Oo-ooh!

Madam! What a saucy question!

But seriously...it always amazes me how people assume novels are autobiographical... It's to underestimate the power of the imagination...erm... you don't have to have done something to write about it . . . .

...I mean Agatha Christie wrote about murder...without – as far as we know- killing anyone...erm...

Right...a question there in the front...

When can we expect a new "Doctor Inchcombe"?

Well.... **Never**, I hope...I think it's time for him to call it a day.... Enough's enough...because, well, ...I'm afraid I'm sick to death of him...sorry folks

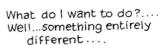

Wow! That's a bombshell for the fans!

! AHhhh

OhH

There's a gust of dismay as though a real death's been announced – which it has in a way. Nicholas killing *our* golden goose, because Dr Inchcombe is as much *mine* as his.

What do I want to do?.... Well...something entirely different....

On stage Nicholas peers in my direction and I know I've made the right decision. I'm going home. And I'll find a good divorce lawyer.

Jody's pissed me off. I'm not speaking to her, texting her or anything. It's ever since Ben (!!) phoned – she's been in La-La Land, totally up herself, thinks she's the cat's knackers.

She never expected him to ring so she never thought things out, that's the trouble. He calls when we're round at Jody's, doing our homework.

Is that Jody?

Yeah

It's Ben... Tamara's friend... she gave me your number

!!!

All I hear is Jody answering Ben's questions with little gaspy "Yes-es", agreeing to look after his dog and telling massive porkies, like she loves dogs, and she's got this nice basket. I mean she hasn't even got a dog bowl. She just assumes she can use my dog's stuff. Afterwards she's like, "Omigod, Casey! What've I done?"

But all she really cares about is meeting Ben, not the dog.

Then just when I need her to help me finish my Maths she wants to celebrate and that pisses me off. Her mum hides the drink these days, but she doesn't know to hide the air duster.

Yay! Result!

I'm meeting him! Me-ee-eeting him, Casey!.....He's so·oo lush!!

Geddoff!!

But what really did it for me was in the evening, at Katie Pound's. I was really getting it on with Ryan (♥ ♥ !) – well not exactly, but he'd just asked me to his birthday party. Jody comes up in this new top, flashing her teapot lids. Need I say more?

...wot you mean it was just a friendly snog?! **Why** do it with **him** if it means nothing??

Dunno... maybe I was getting some practice in...

Well, you're a **bitch**, Jody! Sod off!

WHAT'S THE DIFF BETWEEN BOYZ N CHEESE?
CHEESE MATURES. LOL JODY

KC WOT U UP 2? XXX JODY

KC ANSA ME! XXX J

KC I NEED 2 CU! PLEEZ XX J

Texting is Jody's way of saying sorry.
They keep coming, getting more and
more desperate. So in the end we agree
to meet.
  Turns out she's come down WHAM! to
planet Earth. When Jody asked her mum
if she'd mind having a friend's dog to
stay she goes, Yes she does bloody mind
and gives Jody the Big Grill, like what
was she thinking of, and who's this
friend?

But it's a nice dog, Mum!
...Casey wants to look
after him too...

He'd be company
for me when you're
working...

No, Jody...I
said...I don't
want a dog
here...

But I sort
of said
YES...

Well just ring and
say **NO**...or d'you
want *me* to?...
...what's the number,
eh?

No, Mum
Don't!!!
I'll do it!

Oh just someone
from school....

No, Jody! No way! I'm
not looking after that
dog!...Look, just ring
Ben, say you changed
your mind....
  Godsake forget
this mad fantasy
of yours!

But it's the only fantasy
I've ever had!...only
thing I ever wanted
badly....

I just want to **MEET**
him...tell him forget the
dog...tell him the truth:
I just want to see him...
talk...nothing else......
nothing SEXY...cos I
realise that's a bit off...

Jody won't ring Ben. She won't let me
ring him. She's sort of frozen.
She's mental. She's done totally what
you're not supposed to – she's not only
given her address to a strange bloke but
asked him to visit her tomorrow, while
her mum's still at work.
  Supposing Ben's lairy, weird. Keeps his
dead mum in the freezer? Or a perve –
likes doing gross things to . . .

Go on!
Ring him

...trouble is...
don't want to...

Omigod, the state of Jody, waiting for Ben to come! Every two minutes she's like bottling, "What's he going to say? What's he going to say?" And then she's going, "Stay with me Casey, stay with me!" But then as soon as he comes, I have to leg it, disappear and not even TRY papping him. The whole time Jody's stressing about her look: is it sexy/casual, can I still see her sock marks? Which of her fave books should he find her reading? What message is she giving out? Well. she's wearing tiny ribbon knickers AND leggings, she stinks of J-Lo Love at First Glow, AND fags AND Polo mints. So, well foxy.

Actually she's doing my head in , her and her stupid dramas. She wouldn't ring Ben, wouldn't tell him not to come . . .

Ooh shit, what's gonna happen!!??

What you ***ing think?

Jo-dee! He's coming all the way from London...for you to go "Sorr-ee, can't look after your dog...but how 'bout a chat?"

Think about it!!

He's going to be well **pissed off**...give you a mega-bollocking, then **GO!** . . . . .

Or...OK, OK...say he thinks you're **hot**... ...well, he's not going to be Mr Dewy Eyes

Ben...he's prob'ly met like **nine zillion** groupies...**why**'d he treat you any different? ...you know, five minutes **rub-a-tug**, then he'd go..... **YOU KNOW THAT!**

Look, I don't want to...

Anyway, Ben doesn't come.

We wait hours, all morning, and he doesn't show. Twice, Jody gets his voice mail, but doesn't leave a message. Too uncool. She's really, really gutted. I'm going, "Well, that's how celebs behave. Ben's not A-list any more, but that's what they do. They forget stuff, find more important stuff to do, treat people like total dross." But Jody isn't blaming Ben, she blames this village. She's mad at Ewedown, like Ewedown's whole point is to make life suck, like it's just a nothing, nothing place, up to its arse in mud and grass and stuff. Like it's soundproofed, event-proofed.

Jody wants to be alone. She's got that look she has before she does something, like go on a little cider bender or whatever.

Winnards Farm... ...going to borrow something for Ryan's party tonight...

...I tried to make something **HAPPEN**!!!

HATE this ***ing place!!

Where you going?

Saturday afternoon

Hallo Jody...

OhH!! You!! OHHH.. Ben!

Gave you a shock, did I?

...Guessed you might be along...

?!?

yeah...I guessed **you** might be the somebody who's been getting in here ...pissing about...... Sending e-mails on Tamara's laptop...

Know what I'm saying... don't you?

Dear Ben
Have found really reliable dog-lover in the village who would love to look after Boss. Please deal directly with Jody on 07642 998096.
Tamara

See, when I thanked Tamara for that e-mail...and she replied she **NEVER** sent it, didn't even **KNOW** you...

... Well, didn't take genius to suss who might've...

There was your phone number...so.... thought I'd turn up today...make sure.. and here you are!...What the ✱✱✱✱ you doing !!?...breaking and entering... ...people get in deep shit doing tha....

Didn't **BREAK** in!!... we...I...only did it when the house was empty.... and it was empty all bloody winter!

So that makes it OK, does it? God! *Bloody little pain in the arse you are!*

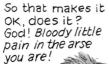

I...I waited for you all morning ....I would've told you....if you'd come to my house.... I... would've told you **EVERYTHING**.....

What EVERYTHING ??
What you on about?

I just...like I always wanted to meet you... just once... ...just to...

...just to tell you stuff...and then...

...like that would be it...

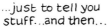

Tell *what?* What *stuff?*

uhLike ... *I love you!*... *I really, really love you!*

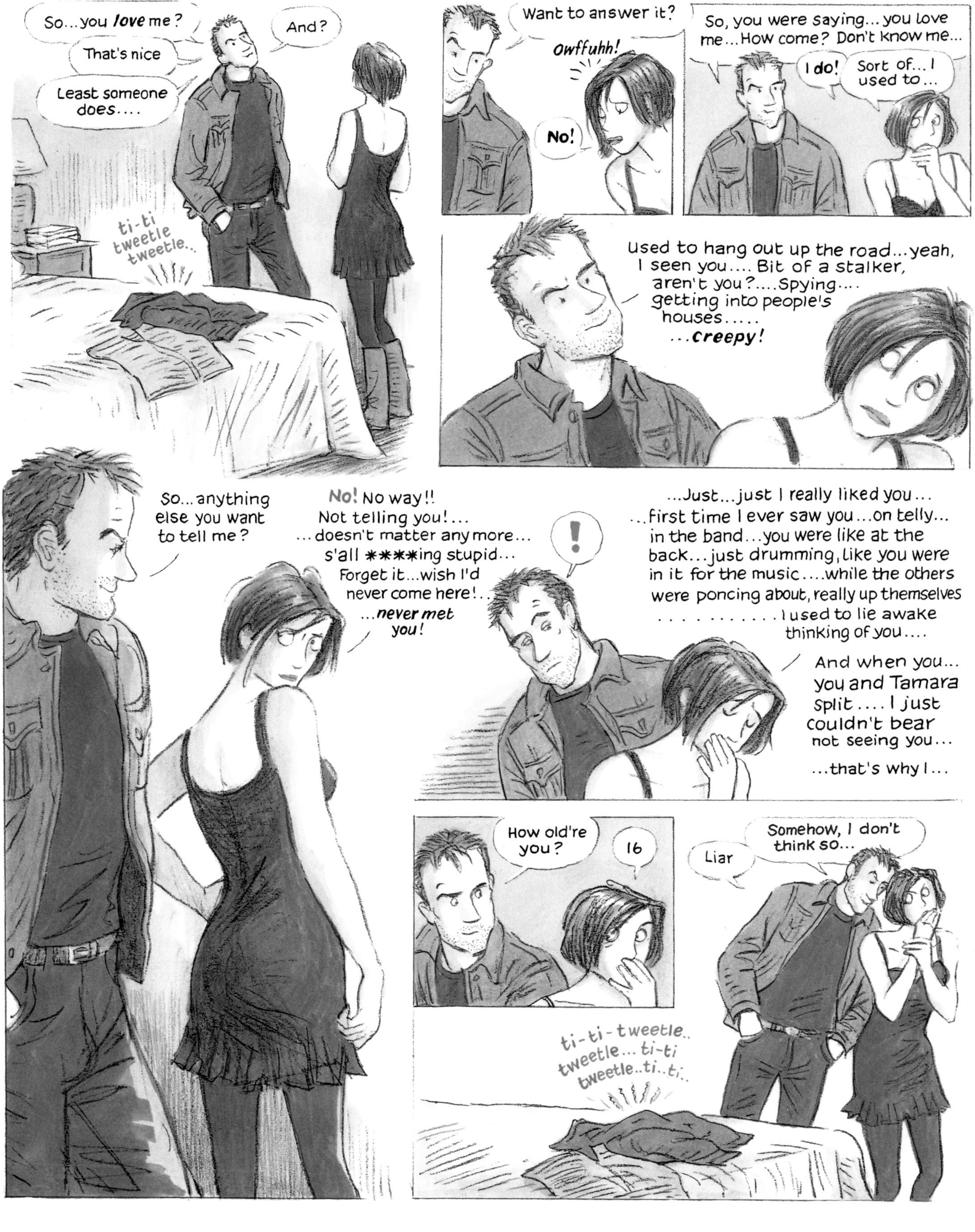

So... you *love* me?
That's nice
Least someone does....
And?
ti-ti tweetle tweetle...
Want to answer it?
Owffuhh!
No!
So, you were saying... you love me... How come? Don't know me...
I do!
Sort of... I used to...
Used to hang out up the road... yeah, I seen you.... Bit of a stalker, aren't you?.... Spying.... getting into people's houses.....
...*creepy!*
So... anything else you want to tell me?
No! No way!! Not telling you!... ...doesn't matter any more... s'all ****ing stupid... Forget it... wish I'd never come here!.. ...*never met you!*
!
...Just... just I really liked you... ...first time I ever saw you... on telly... in the band... you were like at the back... just drumming, like you were in it for the music.... while the others were poncing about, really up themselves .... I used to lie awake thinking of you....
And when you... you and Tamara split.... I just couldn't bear not seeing you...
...that's why I...
How old're you?
16
Liar
Somehow, I don't think so...
ti-ti-tweetle.. tweetle... ti-ti tweetle..ti..ti..

Jody hangs up and I'm like Omigod! She's with Ben at the farmhouse? Maybe getting it on... or what?

Ben's dog is still tear-arsing on the green. When Ben was with Tamara we often saw it on the loose like this, going mental – I suppose 'cos Boss is a London dog and the space freaks him out. I watch till he disappears up the road.

Then Jody rings!! Ben's downstairs at the farm. She can talk, she's jabbering, super-excited: Ben's sussed it's us that's been in the house, but he's cool about it. The MAIN reason he's come today is to pick up some stuff he left at Tamara's. He'll be going soon – well, as soon as his dog comes back. Then Jody goes, "Can you still see the dog? Can you go and catch him and keep him as long as poss?" That's so Jody can have another hour, half hour, ten minutes even, with Ben. I go, "Doing what exactly?" Cos Omigod, sounds like her dream's come true! Was Ben massively loved-up at first sight? Jody goes, "Yeah, he is! Really HOT, all over me."

I go, "He IS?" And Jody goes, "Well, a bit."

But then Jody hangs up. Just like that, suddenly. So I'm like texting...

WHERE KISS? CHEEK? LPS?
WOTKIND? FRENCH? PHLEGMISH?
HAV U LOST YOR V PLATES?
LOL KC

Cate!..haven't rung at a bad time, have I?

What's up, Tamara? Where are you?

Dunno...somewhere near Oxford ...I'm just trying to prolong the journey...can't face getting home.

Nick?... Oh he's.

Oh probably nearly back by now...about to face the music with his wife ¿ GULP ¿

God! It's awful, Cate! He's adamant...he's going to leave her!

She **knows** about Nick and me! She came to his event at the festival...

They didn't speak...but...

...But last night she texted him...and sent some images of **us** together!....said she'd been sent them.... anonymously !!!

And that **DID** it! Nick was totally... totally appalled !!

No, not the PICTURES!.... with HIMSELF!

¿ unhh ¿...squalid... ...unhh ¿

Tamara, I've got to end this...it can't go on...this is **horrible!** I've got to face her... be **honest** for once...

I'm such a **shit!**... ...**total shit**...all our marriage..... treating her like... It's got to **END!!** I can't go on using her!.....lying to her... I've got to leave ....

It's **you** I love !! I want to live with **you**, Tamara !

Whatever happens tomorrow....after I've seen Beth, **promise** me you'll be there...at the farm...in the evening... I'll come to you...... Promise...**promise** you'll be there?

Yes...I promise

I didn't want this to happen....

God, I feel awful...for her...for their kids... – I *know* they're grown up...but...

My only hope is Beth **MAKES** him stay... cos, apparently, she's done that in the past with other girl friends..... ...you know, forgive and forget...

I mean, they've survived **25** years together...*surely* they *wouldn't* split over....

And anyway, *why* would he *want to* leave her?...She's the ideal wife...all the stuff she does for him...

I mean, I can't cook like that ....I couldn't run his life for him, like she does....

Nor do I want to...

So what do you want, Tamara?...thought you loved him...

I do...but...I never thought it would last...it's been too much fun...it's been perfect...just too good to last...

Dunno how it's happened....

..one minute we're having this wonderful, sexy, secret thing – and I can't tell you *how* sexy it's been...

...and the next....

...TOTAL **NIGHTMARE!**

Glen: Saturday afternoon

Beth seems slightly frazzled because she's single-handed. It's another Crime Writing Weekend, seven aspirant authors are here, Mary has the 'flu and Nicholas isn't back yet from wherever. Tomorrow he's supposed to run some kind of workshop.

   Of course, I've helped out, brought wine from the cellar, scraped potatoes, laid the fire in the Reading Room – Nicholas's chores, not that I've ever seen him do them. Not that I see him at all. Our paths cross occasionally out walking, and sometimes in the house on my visits to the toilet.

...it's weird how you go back to what you wrote at the beginning of the book...and you just want to start over.....

Hallo there, Glen....quite part of the family, now....
...book going all right?....

My book is going fine and before too long it's going to wipe the condescending smile off that bastard's face. The only reviews Nicholas gets are little bitty things in crime sections whereas my baby should receive serious critical attention. *Favorable* attention, according to my editor, although she didn't sound so pleased when I told her I have to rewrite the middle section. Means publication is delayed until the spring. But hey, this book has to be good.

   I sit and think over my strategy for the coming months.

   I plan to use London as a base: for teaching, for LIVING, for the buzz and jungle heat which germinates ideas. Stonefield will be for the half-life of writing. I know some people can write under gunfire or while breast-feeding or in heaving Irish bars, but I can do it only in these conditions, conditions I would otherwise scorn: this snug, smug little set-up, everything mild and mannerly – weather, landscape, people.

   I look out at the soft greens and contemplate a stroll. If the rain holds off.

...what if Tamara wants a baby?....

Huh! If she has a baby, she'll find out!! He doesn't **DO** children, Nicholas doesn't! He'll leave *everything* to her...like he did with ours...

But supposing he **doesn't**...supposing he discovers **FATHERHOOD**?....they **DO**, these men, second time round...get all hands on...**nappy-happy**....
...they can't get involved **enough**!

...Just the ultimate insult to me and the children...
God!...if he does that, I'll...

Beth! It's really hard to write with **THAT** going on...

Hey Beth! There's a dog crapping on your lawn!

Ben's dog! God! Means he must be around!

Belongs to Ben ...Tamara's ex. Suppose he's come to beat the shit out of Nicholas *SIGH*

Pardon me, Beth?

Glen...I think you should know... since it may affect you indirectly...

I'm asking Nicholas for a divorce...

It means Stonefield will go on the market...

Oh? !!!

You see, Nicholas is having an affair ...with Tamara...

He *is*? No shit!

God, but listen, Beth!... is that a reason to napalm your *whole life*??!...I mean...

...I mean, OK...this is none of my damn business...but you've been here before, right?...Last fall—it was kinda public, I couldn't help knowing — Nicholas cheated...uh...you forgave him... Yeah?

Yes

OK, so why not let it go this time.... probably it won't last...Tamara will get tired of him...give him the push like his last lover did....uh...

What?

For your information, it was *Nicholas* who ended that affair... ...for my sake...for the sake of our marriage.

Is that what he told you, huh?

Without thinking, I launch straight into the phone call I'd overheard in the toilet, months ago. I watch Beth take it in: Nicholas returned to her only because Nadia didn't want him.

How could you, Glen? ...you've sat in my kitchen all these months...and all the time you knew that.....

...it wasn't my business to...

Certainly made it your business *NOW!*

Excuse me... I must see to that dog...

I go to my barn and stay there. What a bastard I am. A dumb bastard too. I've not only upset Beth but made it a thousand times more likely she'll divorce, sell up, and totally screw my book. *Why* did I tell Beth? Maybe it was just too irresistible, the chance to empty a pail of shit over Nicholas. Maybe it was the shock of having my plans ruined. Stonefield is the only place I can write. My book's unfinished! Goddam Nicholas, why couldn't he keep his pants buttoned?

No sign of Ben's dog in the village, so I walk up towards Winnards Farm and there's Gary, Terry and Nipper sneaking along by the hedge. Usually when they hang out out here it's because the bull's in the field – massively loved-up, getting it on with the cows, etc. But he's not there today, so the boys're bunging clods at the cows. Well, not at them, but near them. And the cows are well pissed off.

MMUHH!

I'm just about to ask them if they've seen a boxer dog when there's barking coming from over the other side of the field. Definitely Ben's dog. Because of the cows I have to leg it all the way round. Towards the woody bit near Stonefield the barking gets louder.

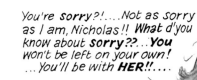

At first I get my phone out 'cos it looks really juicy. Beth and Nicholas! Jody'd want to see this. So I take a few paps. But then it gets so horrible. I never seen anyone so totally lose it like that, for real, not telly. I seen my mum upset, but this is just awful. Beth's mouth like a black O and her voice like an animal trying to get out.

"Glen told me, Glen told me! You lied about Nadia! Even when you want to tell the truth, you li-iie. you li-iie," she's sobbing.

  I start shaking. I can't watch.

Please go!!!...don't want to see you right now!...Go on, go!...go to Tamara...she's there, isn't she?! Go to her! Go on!....

Beth I....

Wough!

And **YOU!! GO HOME!! BUGGER OFF!!!**

...oh God...oh God... ....uhh...

6.30pm

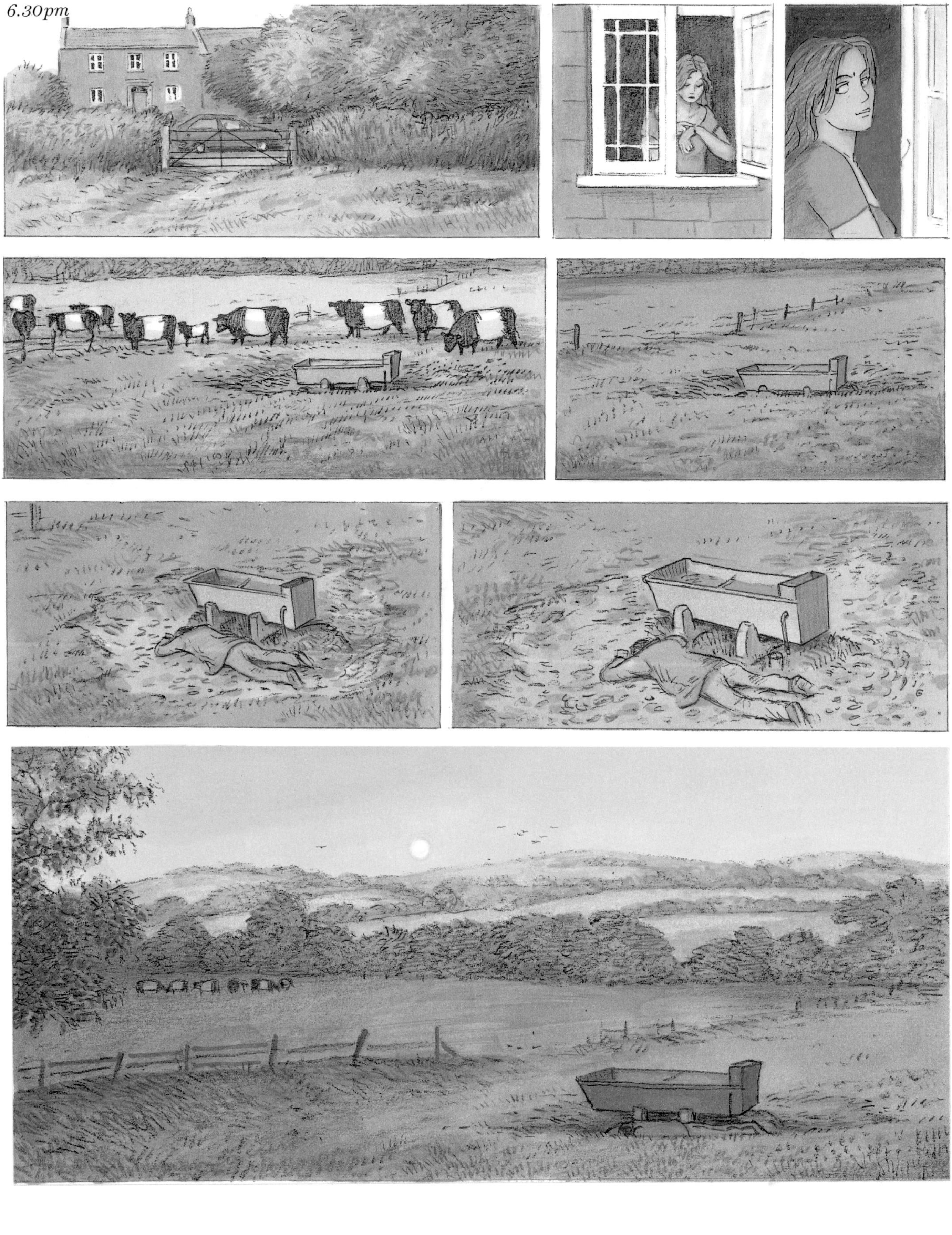

Cate, he **begged**!...Nick *implored* me to be here!..and I *was*!!...at 6·30...I've been waiting **HOURS**!

He doesn't show, doesn't call...doesn't answer his mobile...

Must've decided to stay with his wife, after all...*bastard!* So *much* for his not being able to live without me!....

But Tamara!! That's what you *wanted!* You didn't want to split them up...you should feel relieved!

I **AM**!...but I also feel bloody *insulted*!

He couldn't come round and tell me to my **FACE**, could he?!...*bastard!* ...Couldn't end things that way!....

No, he has to **DROP** me...stand me up...

...cos it soothes his bloody male ego to think *he's* doing the loving and leaving....*bastard!*......... ....*why* did he have to give me all that shit about loving me...? ...why did he..?

God I'm so pissed off, Cate! And there's **NOTHING** to drink!...Bloody Ben was here sometime today and he's drunk the wine! ✱✱✱✱ing **MEN**!...I need a *drink*!

I'd go down the pub, if I..

Sure I can't get you..?

Yes, Andy! I'll get my own... I'm not stopping

Large Rioja please

What's up?

Nothing.

I get off with Ryan at his party! It's like the most amazing thing ever, cos I was doing none of the stuff they tell you in mags. Like I wasn't Creating Intimacy, Listening, Smiling, Asking Questions, Triggering his Me-button, etc.

No, I'm looking really really rank: my hair's crap and I'm having to stand with my back to people cos the only clean thing I could find to wear was these jeans – dead uncomfy, hungry-bum ones. I'm feeling really horrible too. Some of it's to do with watching the Hardimans' screaming match this afternoon. Wish I hadn't. It's like I nicked something. It was also a bit sort of gross, me and Jody looking forward to them having a row. And now they have, a mega one.

I need to talk to Jody! And that's the other thing. I must've dropped my phone in the wood, so we can't ring each other! And where IS she? She hasn't showed up. She's not here. What's she DOING?

The last time we spoke was on my mum's phone hours ago . . .

Where are you, Jody? Ben still around?

He's about to go... ...his dog just came back.... ...he's putting his stuff in the car...

Oh Casey! He's *so·oo nice!*...we've had some wine...he really talked to me....about like what I want to do after school....he's so *nice!*...

...gave me this really nice kiss goodbye...

What else...?... feel your fun-bags?

Yes...I mean, NO!... He's dead, dead scared of me being underage ....

Oh, but it's been brilliant...I'm so *happy*, Casey!...

see you later

I wanted to tell Jody all about Beth and Nicholas and how awful I was feeling. But she didn't want to know. She was all Ben this and Ben that. I've heard Jody being moony before, but never like this, like she and Ben were up to their bums in bluebirds and stuff. I'm thinking maybe this is Dream Come True, maybe she's eloped with Ben. They've run away!!

Ryan's been standing there porking out on Quavers, so I ask if I can use his moby.

Jody not coming, then?

Dunno...just get her voicemail.... Maybe she's not ...

Good

Why *good?*

Cos you two..you're always together!... Can never talk to you

Ryan really wants to talk, or that's what he says. But you can't with the heavy metal blasting away. Inside the house it's like total sweat-box, all armpit, fags and Lynx and everyone starting to snog and fall over. So far what usually happens hasn't happened yet – like older boys crashing the party, bringing drugs and stuff. Maybe this is because Ryan's dad's out the front having some beers with his uncle – who does weights.

Ryan and me, we go out the back into the lane where it smells more of lilac, etc. My heart's jumping and I'm going, "Is this for real or what?"
When Ryan throws his ciggie down, I throw mine down too.

It's like you have to live in this village to understand that an ambulance coming here is like a mega, mega event . . .

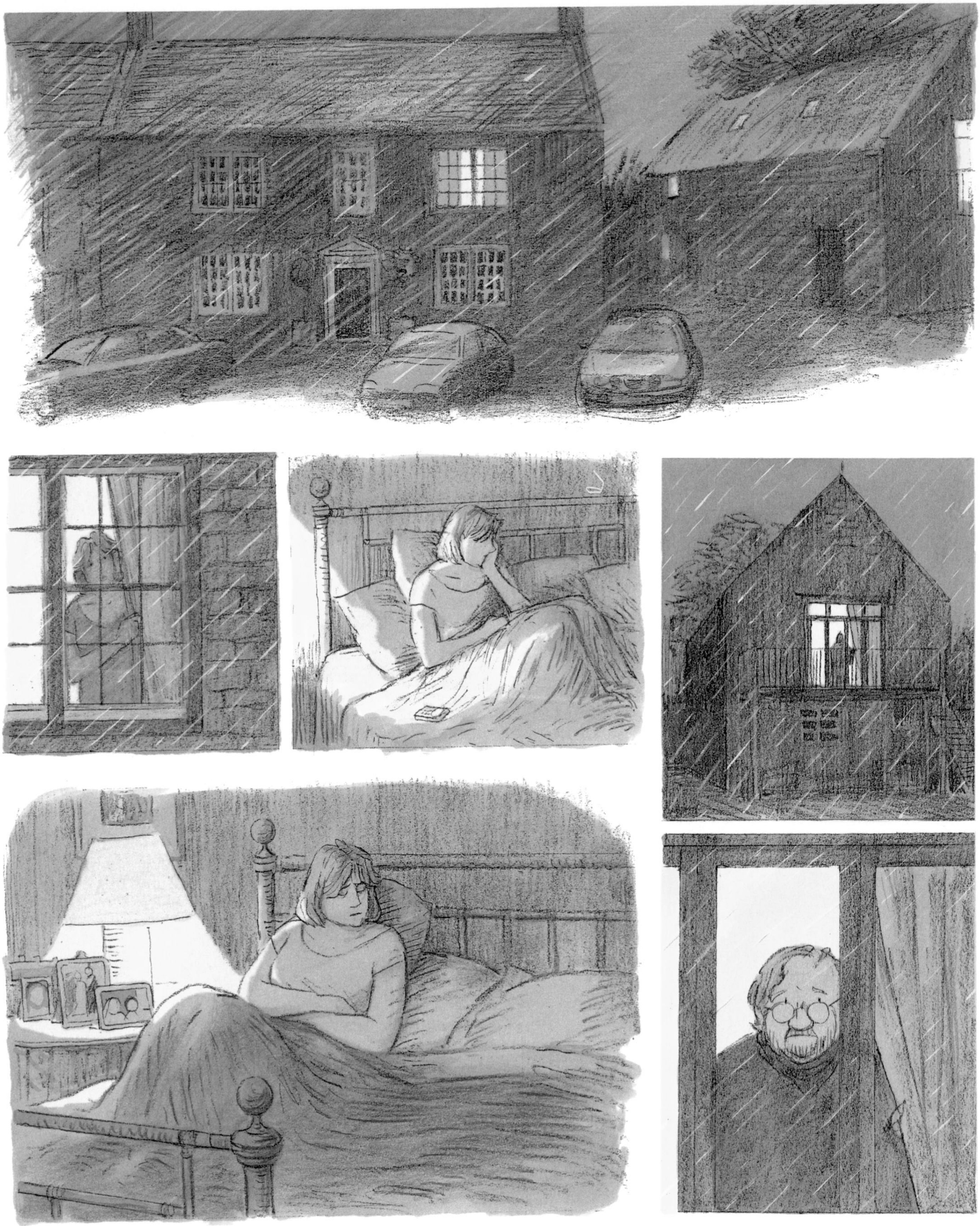

Sunday morning

As soon as I got to Jody's house last night I knew that something really really bad had happened to her. Elaine from number 7 was by Jody's front door. She called into the house, and called my mum's name. My mum came running out, said to me, "You mustn't come in, come home with me". She told Elaine to stay with Jody's mum and told Ryan to go back home too.

I was going, "What's happened, what's happened?" And I was thinking all kinds of stuff, like Ben had raped and murdered Jody, or upset her so she took an overdose or something. But I didn't say it, I didn't want to mention Ben at all. Anyway, the last time I spoke to Jody she was so HAPPY about him.

We went home and we were in the kitchen, Mum, my stepdad and me, whispering a bit so as not to wake my little sister.

See, Jody's mum went upstairs to find out why she hadn't gone to the party... and there she was... on the bed...**DEAD**...Jody still had the spray can in her hand...

I told Mum a bit about Jody doing the air duster, like it gives you a little buzz. It's not illegal like drugs and it's just stuff people have lying around for their PCs.

Then Mum wanted to know if I did it and I said no, which is gospel – I was too chicken.

I didn't tell about anything else. On and off Jody always tried things – huffing, waccie-baccie, etc. She does it for kicks or when she's bored or she wants to celebrate. Last night it would have been to celebrate... her time with Ben. I KNOW it would.

A police car goes up the road, then an ambulance. For a moment I have a flash it's bringing Jody back. She'll get out and be her gobby little self again and all this will be a dream.

Beth:

Three of the crime writers found Nicholas – including Lynda, who'd been so cross at dinner last night when he didn't show up. They'd been for an early morning walk in the fields and found his body by the cattle trough.

The police came. Two officers this morning and a plainclothes detective in the afternoon. Andy suggested I might have said the wrong thing. But what is the right thing to say when you're told your husband's dead, seemingly trampled by Penny Upmaster's cows? I was so shocked I immediately said it was my fault because I set the dog loose. I let bloody Ben's dog go and it must have panicked the herd. It was my fault. The policewoman said the post mortem would "ascertain the facts".

Andy came with me to identify Nicholas. He propped me up. Poor Nicholas. And the poor children. I can't bear it for them. That was almost the worst, phoning Fred in Cairns, telling Lulu, going to pick her up from the station. And all the rest of the family. Getting Nick's sister to tell his mother. Telling his agents, his publisher, before they heard it on the news.

Who haven't I rung?
I must unfreeze the moussakas for the family tomorrow.
Poor Nicholas. I can't bear it.
Poor Nicholas.

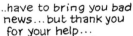

I answer a few questions. So do all the crime writers, before they make their tactful getaway from Stonefield.

I confirm that Ben's dog was around on Saturday and that I know it had chased cows before. I say I don't know if the cattle are aggressive. I've always avoided them. They look mean bastards, but then all cows stare at you. As far as I'm concerned, the Hardimans' relationship is one of affectionate cooperation. No, I didn't hear them arguing before Nicholas went off. Beth seemed her usual busy self on Saturday. (A lie. Beth was fuming, and what I told her would have made her madder than ever with Nick.)

I can't think what to do. My brain isn't working. I seem to spend a lot of time by the window. I feel awful. I should speak to Beth.

Mum finds girl dead

A TEENAGE GIRL was found dead at a house near Hadditon at about 9pm on Saturday. Jody Long, 15, was discovered in her bedroom by her mother Pam, 43. According to one report Jody died after inhaling from an aerosol canister which was still in her hand.

Next door neighbour Elaine Porter said she saw the teenager on her way home around 6pm. She said, "Jody was all smiles, bursting with life", and added, "It's a terrible tragedy. I just can't believe it. Everyone here is in shock".

A post mortem was due to take place yesterday in Brueminster.

Last few days my stepdad goes and buys loads of papers from the service station at Fourways. Jody's been in them. At first, not on the front page or on national telly like Nicholas Hardiman, but just small mentions, plus our headmaster said things about her on local news. At school we had special assembly, everyone gutted and hugging. At home Mum and Paul treat me like I've been really ill and try not to upset me with questions. Which is like a relief cos I'm feeling so totally crap about Jody and Jody's mum Pam. She comes round to us a lot and I can't look her in the eye. I know she'll never ever say it, but she must be sort of thinking, if I knew Jody was inhaling stuff, why didn't I tell someone and she might still be alive?

Course, there have been questions. I was really shitting myself when the policewoman came round. I thought she was going to ask about the Armani dress Jody was wearing, where she'd thieved it. Then, unless I told massive porkies, it'd all have come out – us getting in the farm, taking Tamara's stuff, Ben, etc. But the police only asked, how did Jody seem on Saturday, did she do other drugs, did she know the dangers?

So it wasn't me who dragged Ben into the papers. Jody's mum did. She showed the police the demo disc he gave Jody, along with a Post-It note with Ben's autograph and Saturday's date. Plus, Ben's phone number was on Jody's moby. That's how Ben got interviewed and that's how all the papers started sort of joining up the dots between Jody, Ben , Tamara and Nicholas Hardiman. Ewedown's in the news! The pub's full of journalists, there's telly crews everywhere, it's MENTAL!

Daily Post

WHO WANTS TO MILLIONA £90m JACKI

'Dr INCHCOMBE' A FOUND DEAD FIELD

Cows suspected of trampling popular author Nicholas Hardiman

Jody love Ben Sergeant may 28

Ben Sergeant said last night he had arranged with his ex-girlfriend Tamara Drewe to pick up sor belongings from the £1.3 millic farmhouse, "She left a key unde a pot. While I was there my dog wandered off."

Sergeant stated that he had met Jody Long by chance, while waiting by his car for the dog to return. "She was a big Swipe fan. We chatted for 20minutes. Then my dog came back and I left for London".

Author's sex tryst led to tragedy

Pop star Ben last to see tragic Jody

Swipe drummer quizzed over teen's death

Evening Advertiser

1000 CELEBS AWARDS

ROCK STAR SHARED S LOVER AS TRAGIC AUT

Girl friend of Swipe drummer had secret affair with dead author, Nicholas Hardiman

SALE

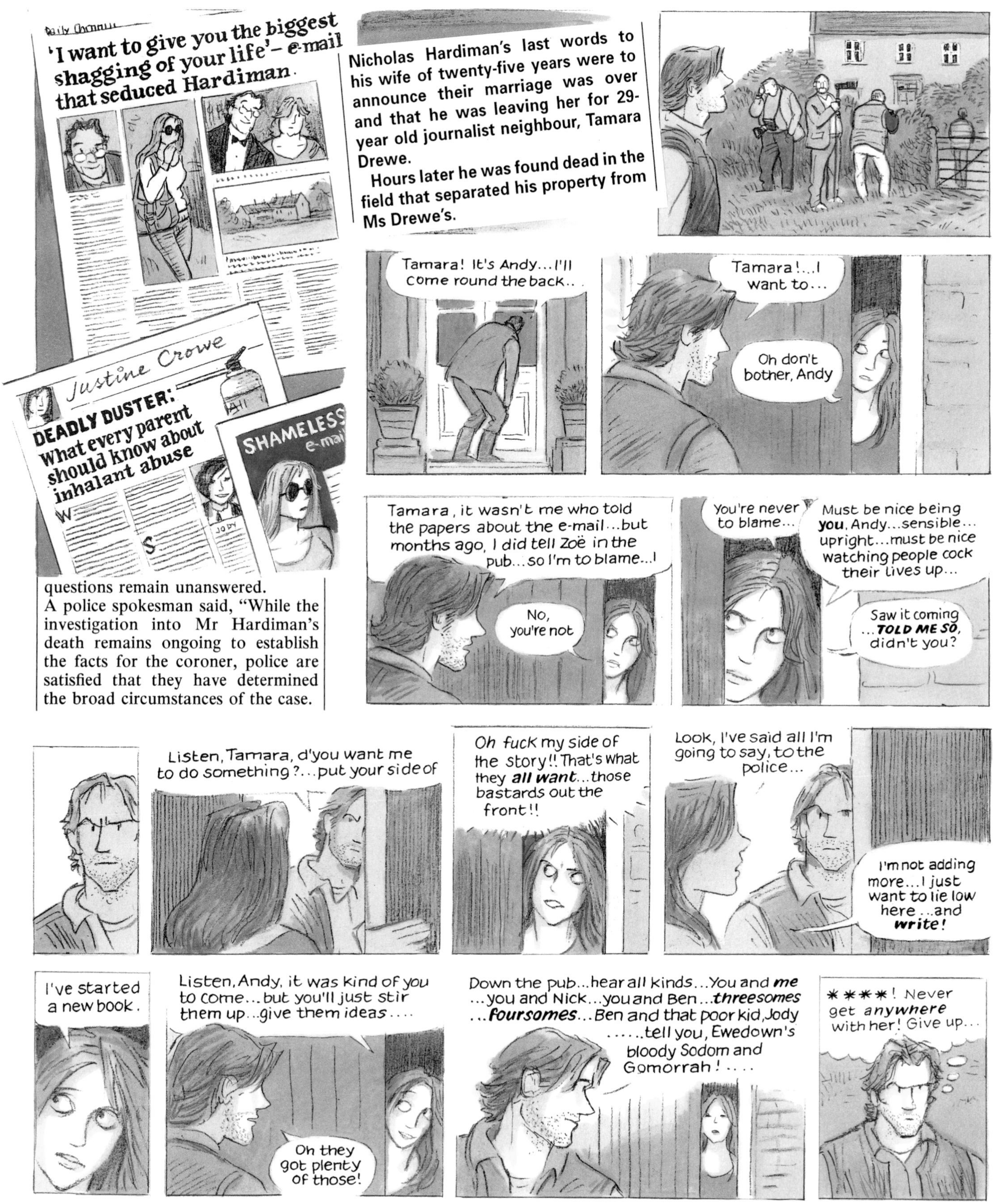
Daily Chronicle
'I want to give you the biggest shagging of your life'– e-mail that seduced Hardiman.
Nicholas Hardiman's last words to his wife of twenty-five years were to announce their marriage was over and that he was leaving her for 29-year old journalist neighbour, Tamara Drewe.
Hours later he was found dead in the field that separated his property from Ms Drewe's.
Justine Crowe
DEADLY DUSTER:
What every parent should know about inhalant abuse
SHAMELESS
e-mail
JODY
questions remain unanswered.
A police spokesman said, "While the investigation into Mr Hardiman's death remains ongoing to establish the facts for the coroner, police are satisfied that they have determined the broad circumstances of the case.
Tamara! It's Andy...I'll come round the back..
Tamara!...I want to...
Oh don't bother, Andy
Tamara, it wasn't me who told the papers about the e-mail...but months ago, I did tell Zoë in the pub...so I'm to blame...!
No, you're not
You're never to blame...
Must be nice being you, Andy...sensible...upright...must be nice watching people cock their lives up...
Saw it coming ...TOLD ME SO, didn't you?
Listen, Tamara, d'you want me to do something?...put your side of
Oh fuck my side of the story!! That's what they all want...those bastards out the front!!
Look, I've said all I'm going to say, to the police...
I'm not adding more...I just want to lie low here...and write!
I've started a new book.
Listen, Andy, it was kind of you to come...but you'll just stir them up...give them ideas....
Oh they got plenty of those!
Down the pub...hear all kinds...You and me ...you and Nick...you and Ben...threesomes ...foursomes...Ben and that poor kid, Jody .....tell you, Ewedown's bloody Sodom and Gomorrah!....
****! Never get anywhere with her! Give up...

For short bursts of time I work like crazy on my book. Suddenly I just have to finish. To hell with reworking the middle section, to hell with pussying around. Life's too short. I want to get shot of the bastard. I want to go back to London. Back to Maggie.

Then my concentration vanishes and I'm drawn at once to the windows. Over the past days there's been a lot of *va et vient* – grieving family and friends, deliveries of flowers and mail and journalists trying their luck. One awful time I see Lulu weeping in the garden with Beth. No funeral yet while the cops continue to cover the bases. Two days ago a finger seemed to point at Ben, Tamara's ex, who has a fine motive for bumping off his rival. But then CCTV images at a gas station prove that Ben was where he said he was at the time. The death is understood to be from multiple injuries inflicted by the cows and a collision with the water trough.

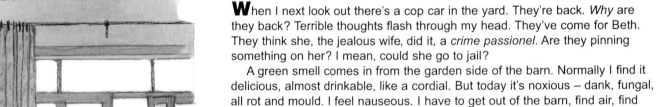

Nicholas would have been pleased with the media coverage: the public shock, the tributes and the many long and fulsome obituaries. "Survived by his wife Beth and his children, Lulu and Fred," they say. They don't say, "Survived by the hot babe he was screwing." But Tamara is all over the Press, the siren and temptress who lured Nicholas to his death.

When I next look out there's a cop car in the yard. They're back. *Why* are they back? Terrible thoughts flash through my head. They've come for Beth. They think she, the jealous wife, did it, a *crime passionel*. Are they pinning something on her? I mean, could she go to jail?

A green smell comes in from the garden side of the barn. Normally I find it delicious, almost drinkable, like a cordial. But today it's noxious – dank, fungal, all rot and mould. I feel nauseous. I have to get out of the barn, find air, find a big open space,

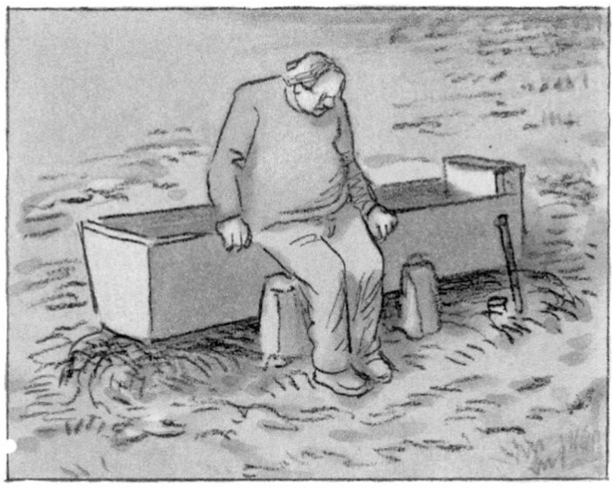

I find myself by the water trough. The mud has dried out and my feet don't sink in like they did the day Nicholas died.

I've lied. After I told Beth about Nadia I didn't go to my barn. I took a walk, the walk I've just done. It avoids the cows, but at one point the path skirts the field, and that's where Nicholas had spotted me that fateful afternoon . . .

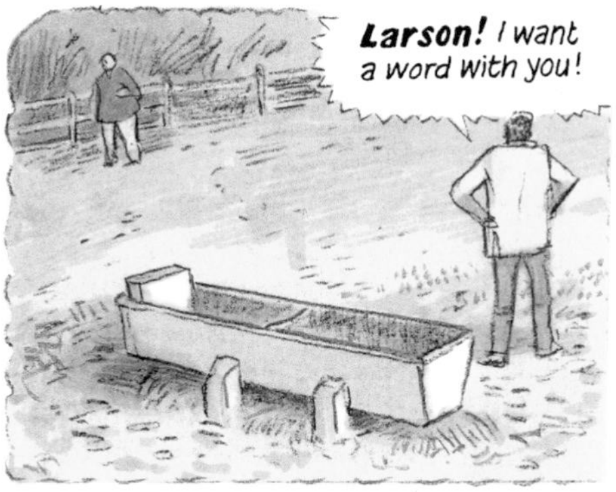

Larson! I want a word with you!

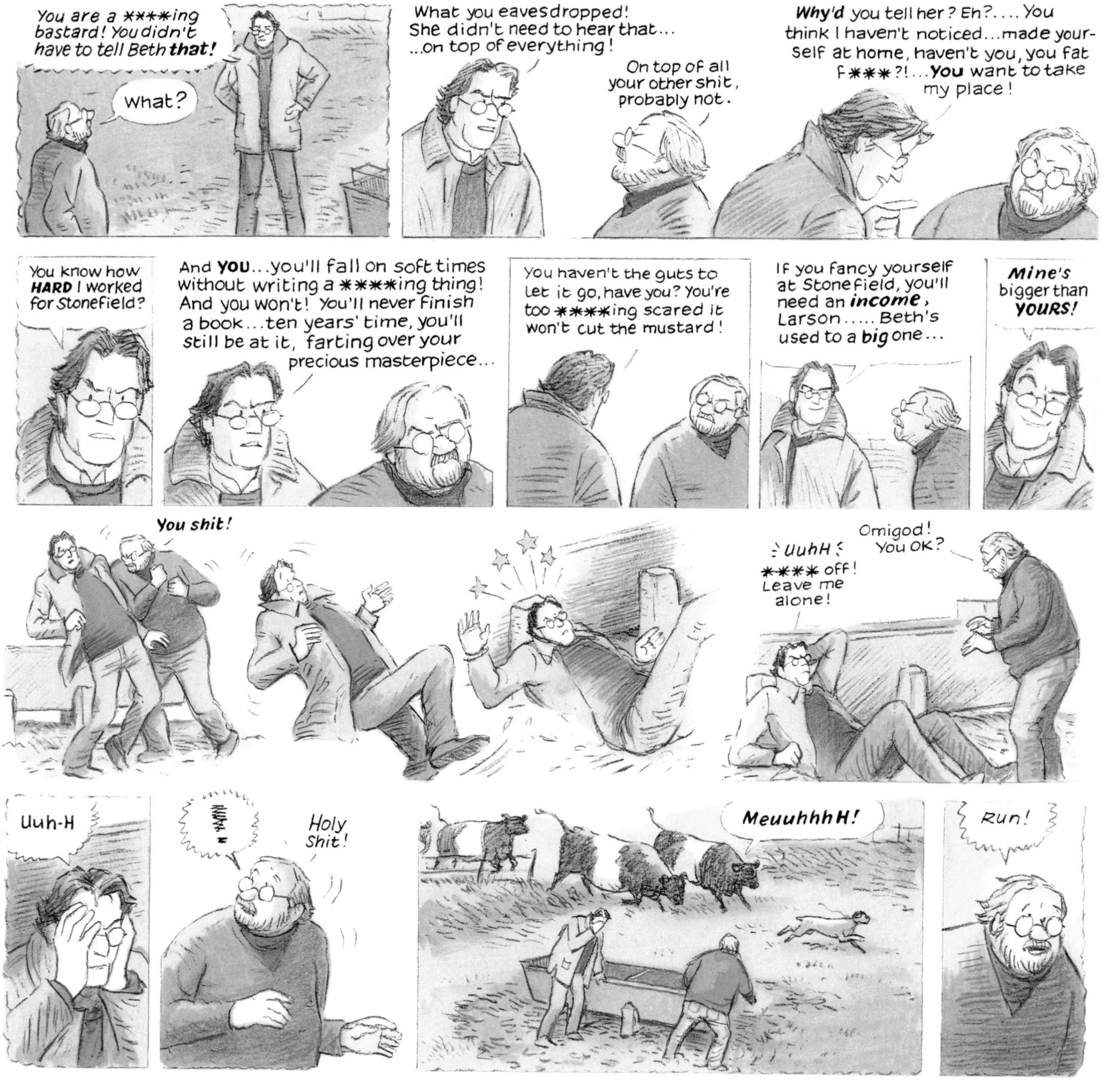

You are a ****ing bastard! You didn't have to tell Beth that!
What?
What you eavesdropped! She didn't need to hear that... ...on top of everything!
On top of all your other shit, probably not.
Why'd you tell her? Eh?.... You think I haven't noticed...made yourself at home, haven't you, you fat f***?!...You want to take my place!
You know how HARD I worked for Stonefield?
And YOU...you'll fall on soft times without writing a ****ing thing! And you won't! You'll never finish a book...ten years' time, you'll still be at it, farting over your precious masterpiece...
You haven't the guts to let it go, have you? You're too ****ing scared it won't cut the mustard!
If you fancy yourself at Stonefield, you'll need an income, Larson..... Beth's used to a big one...
Mine's bigger than YOURS!
You shit!
UuhH
**** off! Leave me alone!
Omigod! You OK?
Uuh-H
Holy Shit!
MeuuhhhH!
Run!

Making for the fence I was aware the dog seemed to be enjoying it, of how he dodged and swerved and doubled back. I just kept on going homewards, and never questioned why Nicholas wasn't following me. I figured he wouldn't want more of my company, that he'd go to Tamara's house along with the dog.

I figured wrong. He must have been too dazed to run from the mad cows. He might have slipped in the gloopy mud, he might have . . .

Well, that's what has run through my head ever since – that and coming clean about pushing Nicholas over. Or not coming clean about it.

I don't hear Tamara approach. First thing I know is her soothing voice and my shoulder being rubbed. It's all too much.

NuhUhh!

God . . . you OK? What's the matter? Whatever is it?

UhhH!

Something happened . . . didn't it? . . . Is it really that bad? . . .

What is it? Sometimes if you put it into words . . . it makes it clearer . . . .

What happened, Glen? You can tell me . . . .

!

Pardon me? . . is this an interview?

Excuse me . . .

Back at Stonefield the cop car has gone. I meet Mary, who's about to drive Lulu into town. She tells me I'll find Beth in the garden. A good thing it's the garden, a large and neutral space for the grenade I may launch.

I'm immediately struck by how much happier Beth looks.

Hi!

Glen! You *must* read this!

AWAY FROM IT ALL

by Tamara Drewe

Cherchez les femmes!

Whenever a malefactor hits the headlines, whether, murderer, molester or minister with his pants down, he won't be alone in the glare of publicity. It's no good his wife, his mum, his mistress trying to keep their heads down. Step forward ladies. If he's a bad'un, it's all your fault.

You went out to work and neglected him or you stayed at home and smothered or you're too sexy or you're not sexy enough.

I could go on. It's always the women that get the stick. Me included. Readers may have noticed, I am the "leggy mistress" of the late creator of "Doctor Inchcombe", guilty of the oldest crime in the book, provoking men, leaving them utterly defenceless. I don't ask for sympathy. I am to blame for having seduced a married man. But is his wife to blame merely for being plump and over 50? Judged by all the unflattering photographs, she is. "Let herself go, no wonder he strayed." That's the subtext. I say, leave her alone!

As for another case in the story, the mother of tragic teen Jody Long is blamed : a single parent, a working mother, so obviously a bad mother. No mention of her absent husband.

Suppose that's one way of dealing with a guilty conscience.

Beth tells me her good news. The police are now convinced Nicholas's death was an accident and have closed the investigation. There remains the limbo waiting for the coroner's report and the release of the body. But the finger of suspicion is no longer pointing anywhere.

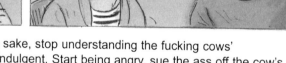

The accident I can sort of handle...if I see it in terms of natural cause and effect..

um..I mean I don't blame the cows...

...I mean we live in the country...we share it with large animals...who aren't wallpaper...who freak out like *we* do, when we're threatened... ...it's a risk we run...

I want to yell at Beth. God's sake, stop understanding the fucking cows' point of view, stop being so indulgent. Start being angry, sue the ass off the cow's owners, or . . . . then I think, OK, this is the way she copes.

For me, confession and silence hang in the balance. I choose silence, chicken out and say nothing about my fatal shove. The cows have taken the rap for killing Nicholas. The world would say I spared Beth the details to save my skin and because I have a book to finish. Of course I'll go away and hate myself and have my guts eaten away with guilt. Useful for a writer, folks would also say. I tell myself it's out of compassion that I keep quiet. Beth will always carry an image of her husband's death. Isn't it better she carries *her* version, the one she seems able to bear?

In a moment I'll go to the barn and begin packing my things. Tomorrow morning I'll leave Stonefield. I've a feeling I won't be back.

Mum and Paul have bought a book about drugs, so they've got the knowledge, can talk the talk, go on about scag, buda, snowtoke, hotloads and stuff. Plus they know all the SIGNS. The sign for what Jody huffed is a numb tongue – well one of the signs, anyway. I overheard Mum say they'd done tests on Jody for other drugs and if like she'd had sex with Ben the other day. She hadn't. (I could've told them that.) Anyway it's like definite the aerosol did her. So now Jody's funeral's going to be soon. In church, over at Aldwick St Mary.

    Yesterday I got my phone back. Ryan went and found it cos I was bottling about going anywhere near Stonefield. It was there, down by the gatepost where I thought I'd dropped it. Massive relief or what! Ryan's being really super-nice hanging out with me instead of his boy mates. OK, we do have a bit of snog action but a lot of the time it's just talking about stuff. The bus shelter makes me think of Jody, so we go way, way out in the fields, under a sodding great tree.

    I told Ryan EVERYTHING. About Jody and me getting in Tamara's house, Jody sending the shag e-mail for a laugh.

...but I do!..I feel really bad. cos Tamara's getting grief in the papers about it..like she's a slag....

There's still photographers hanging out round at Winnards Farm... She's **hot** that's why...

What should I do...? **Do?** Do **what??**.... Casey, do nothing, OK? Just keep shtum....

Then I showed the pix I took of Nicholas and Tamara snogging and the ones of him and Beth having a ruck the day he died.

UhhGod I feel sooo awful! Woooo!

Casey, shut it...look, it's tough shit he died...tough shit for his wife...but **you** can't do anything.....**stop** worrying! You don't even **know** them, do you? You ever spoken to Tamara? NO

Just stop worrying.....Ask yourself: would they give a **✳✳✳✳** about **you**, their sort? Would they? NO... Well then

The e-mail arrived this morning.

It was while I was in Hadditon with my daughter. I'd cut Tamara Drewe dead, once by the yoghurts and once in the car park, when Lulu was returning the trolley. Tamara said my name. I ignored her, which wasn't as satisfying as I'd imagined. Afterwards I sat and bit my knuckle in the car. To cheer me up on the way home Lulu gave me a riff from her thesis.

...to the Taliban...so, OK, what's a woman in a burka?...just another **sort** of sex object! Doesn't make men more respectful ...doesn't deal with their fundamental **DISGUST** at being in thrall sexually to inferior beings.... ...They can't give up what they despise...so they **punish** women...

From: Casey Shaw
Sent: 11 May 2006
To: Beth Hardiman
Subject: Apology

Dear Mrs Hardiman
You don't know me but I live near you in Ewedown. This is to say sorry for things I did with my friend Jody which were out of order. It was us that sent you the pictures of your husband and Tamara. It was us that sent the e-mail on her computer which Tamara is getting stick for. We did it for a laugh and because we were bored but we didn't mean any harm. I'm really sorry about your husband. Jody would be too but as you know she's passed away. I've been thinking about this a lot. I hope you can forgive me.
Casey Shaw

I haven't been in the fields since Nicholas's death. They look sinister now and it's hard to adjust – I've always thought of the landscape as being arranged for my personal pleasure: a sort of living calendar, a nice view from every room.

Now I trace Nicholas's steps, walking briskly only glancing at the place where the cows . . . But the cows are elsewhere today and the grass has grown long and lush. At Tamara's gate I nearly turn back. I can't bear it. Nicholas. He would have heard the same rusty squeak, the same leaves would have brushed his arm.

I practically have a nervy-B when I hear it's bloody Beth at the door. I never thought I'd have to meet her, just thought she might reply and hack me off in an e-mail. It's been bad enough getting a bollocking from Tamara, even though it wasn't a mega one, like she didn't scream at me, but more like . . .

..what were you and Jody playing at?!

You did my head in...you really...

I'm sorry...

I couldn't help crying, which is like totally cringey. And now I'm like trying to wipe snot away, and in the hall Tamara's going, "You'd better come in, Beth. Casey's here. She's brought a dress of mine back. I gather she's sent you an e-mail too".

Now it's Tamara's turn to get a bollocking, for having it off with Nicholas. Well, ME too, for what I did. It's really weird standing next to her, Tamara – Jody and my total style-queen – who's got black rings under her eyes and a massive zit.

So....

I'm sorry, Beth ...I'm sorry... What can I say?

I don't think you can say anything ...there's nothing to say..... What's done's **DONE**.....

I don't know why I'm talking to you...you...both of you...you've been incredibly thoughtless...**STUPID**! I should be very **ANGRY!!**

But...I've decided..what's the point?

I've spent far too much of my life hiding anger...being suspicious... resentful...and I can see myself going that way with you...hating you, Tamara... avoiding you, Casey... Snubbing you, cursing you...

What's the point?...stupid weight to carry around...stupid waste of energy....and...in the end, we've all got to live here, haven't we...?

I want to say no, I'VE got to live here, but you and Tamara, you can go to London, or anywhere. But I don't say it. Tamara's blowing her nose and Beth's hand is shaking.

Oh God, I gave up smoking fifteen years ago...but... you haven't got a cigarette, Tamara, have you?

sorry

No...I quit.. *Funny*, I want one too

I have! I've got one left

So then we're sat there the three of us, passing the ciggy around, like Jody and me always did after school.

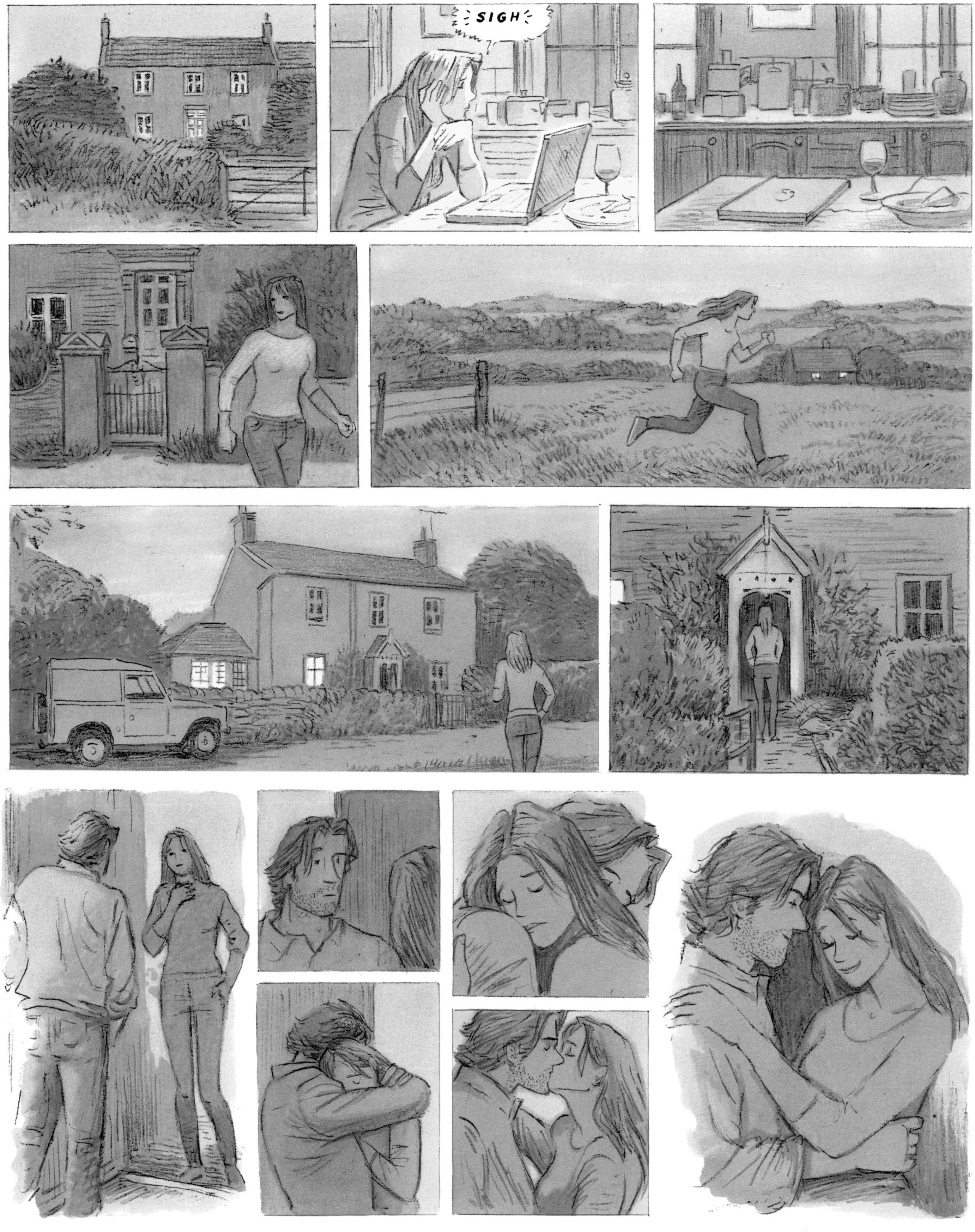
SIGH

Ewedown mourns Jody

TRADE PI

The local paper isn't entirely accurate. A big crowd from all over the district turns out for Jody Long's funeral. But only part of Ewedown pays its respects: Andy Cobb, people from Aspen Close – in other words, the real locals. Not surprisingly, no one was there from up this way, the incomer-weekender part. I didn't attend, although Casey Shaw told me what time and where. I couldn't face a funeral, when Nicholas's hadn't taken place. Besides, I don't know Jody's family. In all these years, we may have nodded from our cars, but that's all.

Tamara Drewe went to the funeral. I know, because something made me walk the mile and three-quarters to Aldwick St Mary. Everyone was milling about before going to the village hall. There was Andy, introducing Tamara. And there was Tamara, all sympathetic smiles. Entrancing people, you could tell. Enviable.

Casey!

Beth!

Oh look!

There's Beth!

I fled. Or rather I pretended not to see her.

I drifted out of sight, away from what I knew was coming: the public hug of Closure. I just can't do that. I can't. I may have ceased hostilities with Tamara, but I'm not on hugging terms.

I'll let her know if I ever am.

One year later

Four magpies this morning in the walnut tree; one for sorrow, a second for mirth, then three for a wedding and four for a birth.

There was plenty of sorrow last year, but now I feel lighter, freer, in charge of my life. Mirth crept back with the return of the writers and the planning of new events at Stonefield – masterclasses, a translators workshop, the award of a young writers' prize in Nicholas's memory.

And there's often mirth these days coming from Nicholas's shed. After I'd cleared it out, sorted and filed everything for the archive, I just couldn't bear to think of another author working in there. So I entrusted Casey Shaw with the key, and now she and the local kids use it as a meeting place. The shed is secluded, far enough from the house, wired, plumbed, double-glazed and so far all the rules – litter, excessive noise, locking up – have been observed. Andy keeps an eye on it.

More mirth. Andy, who spends his life watching things grow, who always knows the best time to plant or pick, chose the right moment to chat up Tamara. He moved in with her at Winnards Farm almost a year ago. He was worried what I would think, but I'd seen it coming. If he's happy, and he seems to be, transforming the garden, expanding his organic veg, then I'm glad. As for Tamara, our relationship is neighbourly, built on mutual aid – borrowing, lending, giving advice. I look over her publishing contract, she sorts out my computer problems; I lend my Rotavator, she lets me use her big scanner.

There's been no wedding or talk of one. But there have been births. Tamara had a baby in January and her first novel comes out in September. (Her notoriety over Nicholas did her no harm, it seems, from the hefty advance.) The baby delights them both. Some people say he's very like Andy, others like his mother. But whenever I see him, I think he has a look of Nicholas about the eyes. Probably my imagination.

Today a fan letter from Beth Hardiman. "Congratulations on the very well deserved success of your novel. It must be very gratifying after all the hard work to receive the perfect combination – terrific reviews and sales. It's very exciting news that it may be turned into a film . . ." Beth is very proud of the part that Stonefield may have played in the gestation of *Excess*, and she looks forward to reserving my room if ever I should want . . . Do I know Tamara Drewe has a novel due out in September? She looks beautiful on the cover, Beth hears. It's all about a writer's retreat . . .

About a WHAT?! *Oh my God, no.*

SWINDON COLLEGE

LEARNING RESOURCE CENTRE

by the same author
MRS WEBER'S DIARY
TRUE LOVE
PICK OF POSY
VERY POSY
PURE POSY
MUSTN'T GRUMBLE
GEMMA BOVERY
LITERARY LIFE

for children
FRED
LULU AND THE FLYING BABIES
THE CHOCOLATE WEDDING
BOUNCING BUFFALO
F-FREEZING ABC